WATER GARD[...]

■ Step-by-Step to Success ■

Brian Leverett

CROWOOD GARDENING GUIDES

First published in 1990 by
The Crowood Press Ltd
Gipsy Lane, Swindon
Wiltshire SN2 6DQ

This impression 1991

British Library Cataloguing in Publication Data
Leverett, Brian
    Water gardens.
    1. Water gardens
    I. Title
    635.9'674

ISBN 1 85223 295 1

Picture Credits
With acknowledgements to Bruce Grant-Braham for the Frontispiece and Figs 2, 5, 6, 8, 10, 16, 27, 29, 41, 42 and 44; Peter Horner for Fig 39; Geoff Moore of Dorset Media Services for the front cover photograph and for Figs 19, 20, 22, 26, 46, 50, 57, 86 and 92; Dave Pike for Figs 13, 32, 52, 53, 55, 56, 63, 64, 66, 67, 68, 69, 70, 73, 78, 80, 82, 83, 88, 95, 97, 98, 99, 107, 110, 112, 113, 114, 115, 116, 117, 118 and 119; Jan and Frank Taylor for Figs 3, 4, 15, 17, 18, 25, 37, 40, 43, 47, 49, 51, 54, 62, 90, 91, 93, 94, 96, 100, 104, 106, 108, 109 and 111; all remaining pictures supplied by the author who is indebted to Dr R. Page and R. Newman MSc.

With thanks to Kennedy's Garden Centre for Figs 82 and 83; Swindon Aquatic for Figs 64, 66, 67, 68, 69, 70, 78 and 80; and Thamesdown Borough Council for Figs 63, 73 and 97.

Colour artwork by Claire Upsdale-Jones

Dedication
To Ann

Typeset by Acorn Bookwork, Salisbury, Wiltshire.
Printed and bound by Times Publishing Group, Singapore.

Contents

Preface   5
Introduction   8
1   Siting the Water Garden   13
2   Building the Pond   29
3   Establishing the Pond   43
4   Plants for Ponds   48
5   Pond Life   66
6   Other Features   80
7   The Water Garden Month by Month   91
8   Indoor Water Gardens   98
9   Propagation   107
10   Problems with the Pond   111
     Appendices   116
     Index   127

Preface

The name 'water garden' is often taken simply to mean a pond, involving the creation of an area where water replaces soil in which can be planted water-lilies and a few irises. The true and effective water garden seeks to exploit nature and make use of the modifications to their basic structure that have arisen in many plants to allow them to survive in a watery world. Just as the cacti and succulents have adapted – reducing their leaves to spines, and allowing their stems to become swollen to store moisture – in order to survive the harsh desert environments, so those plants which colonise wetter areas have also had to adapt, the result being a range of plants from the exquisitely beautiful to the bizarre. For example, in terrestrial plants, roots perform a dual role, of anchorage and as the means by which mineral nutrients enter the system. In water-adapted plants, the roots often perform just the first function, while the nutrients are taken through honeycombed stems. Alternatively, with the floating plants the roots have no anchorage role, but trail in the water and extract any minerals which might be present.

In the natural world there are several different watery environments, and the greatest variance between them comes from the depth of the water. Different species have evolved to exploit the habitat provided by all depths. In water over 6ft (180cm) deep, for example, very little will root, except for a few trees. However, in shallower water, there is a progressive number of plants that will prosper. At one extreme there is the largest of the water-lilies, which grows with its rhizomes in the mud, with the stems and then the flowers breaking the surface. As the water becomes less deep, there is a greater range of plants that will grow. Many of these are species of more familiar land plants which have adapted to the environment, but there is also a range of subjects for the 'in between' areas – the wetland or bog plants, for example, that require sodden soil rather than water.

Fig 2   An attractive irregular pond well stocked with water-lilies.

Fig 1   (Opposite) A layout incorporating both classical and natural elements in a green colour scheme.

Some plants are tolerant of a wide variety of conditions and will grow as bedding plants, providing they are watered fairly frequently. They will survive, but are never likely to prosper well if they are not provided with suitable conditions. This is the most important thing to remember in gardening, and especially in water gardening. Although many terrestrial subjects will flourish, for example, with a good supply of manure, this can be anathema to some water garden subjects, many of which are at home only in the most impoverished conditions. The key to success with many subjects is to create an environment which imitates the natural world in which the plants survive. You will never deceive nature, but you can bend the rules to serve your purpose. The aim of the water gardener has to be to live in harmony with nature.

Water gardening is the creation of a special environment, which holds more than just horticultural pleasures. Animals and insects will visit your pond, and perhaps colonise it, whether you wish them to or not. For far too long we have sought to kill those insects which attack crops, and in the process have killed almost to the point of extinction those insects that are harmless to man and, more importantly, act as predators to the harmful species. This in turn has led to the need for more and more insecticides; without them the pests would reach epidemic proportions. There is a limit to the amount of insecticide you can use; ultimately it will destroy not only the pests but also the pollinating insects without which there would be no food supply. Water gardening is environmentally friendly in that the only insect pests likely to be encountered – aphids – may be removed simply by spraying the plants with water. The pests will fall into the pond, where

Fig 3   A general view of a water garden in late summer.

Fig 4　*A colourful pool with Higoi carp.*

they will serve to satisfy part of the voracious appetite of the fish. This insect, for years thought of as an enemy, is therefore part of a food chain which will support the amphibians, newts, toads and frogs which contribute to the overall charm of the water garden. Nature also provides other attractions, like dragonflies and the caddis fly with its delicate lace wings and strangely encased larvae. Such extra insects will subsequently attract birds. Once you start working *with* nature rather than against it, the rewards are unlimited.

So, the gardener is always part naturalist and part scientist, and nowhere is this more true than in water gardening. The misuse of science has created large-scale problems, yet a lack of knowledge of basic botany is probably also the most frequent cause of failure in most gardens. To avoid the problems that result from ignorance, the underlying principles of plant growth and cultivation have been included in the text. The information should be sufficient for the general reader, but for greater detail on plants and animals you are strongly advised to consult specialist reference books. You will find the extra knowledge rewarding in itself, and it will enable you to extract more pleasure from your water garden.

Introduction

No element in garden design is as versatile as water. It has the ability to create peace and solitude, bestowing an eternal quality to the scene – simply looking at water is restful and relaxing. And should you wish the reverse effect of dynamic vitality, this can be created with the aid of a small pump. The water can be made to circulate, producing waterfalls, fountains and other effects. The pump may be switched on and off (there is no advantage in maintaining the flow of water if there is no one to notice the movement), to create the effect that is most suitable at the time and is fitting to your mood. Endless scope is provided for the person who wishes to include or create design accessories. Man-made ornaments of a variety of shapes, sizes and designs can be added – a windmill, possibly large enough to use as a small

Fig 5   The shape of the pond together with its immediate surroundings determines the effect that it creates.

store, gives you a Dutch landscape, while incorporating rocks gives the archetypal alpine scene. The moving water provides dramatic movement, giving a living sculpture to the design. Once the principle of falling water is appreciated, a further endless range of effects can be produced. Water can be made to pour from a never-emptying vessel, or into a jug or bucket that is critically balanced so that it overturns under the weight of a certain volume.

Water allows you to introduce a whole new environment into the garden, which is far easier to control than the garden itself. You can house a variety of fish, from the familiar goldfish to koi carp in their many varieties and forms, and if the area you choose can be given over to nature, then birds, butterflies, caddis-flies, dragonflies, frogs, toads and newts can visit, or stay and perhaps breed.

Water has a fascination all of its own which it is impossible to define. Study a group of people travelling around a large garden open to the public; initially they will take in every detail of the beds, but their appetite for this type of horticulture will rapidly become jaded, their interest only being reawakened when they come to water. Here they will stop, take in the form of design and their eyes will become locked upon fishes darting amongst the vegetation. They will notice the strange forms of plants from the very primitive ferns amongst the first plants to grow on the planet to the almost rhubarb-like appearance of the mighty gunnera which has the largest flower of any plant on earth. They will see the rose-like flowers of the water-lily in the purest colours and the rich blooms of the globe flower or *Trollius* that only grow in the damp of the bog garden. Even as children we are fascinated by ponds and the natural history that they attract, how many days in the countryside have been enlivened by a search for fish, newts or tadpoles? The love of water in its natural habitat or a scene created to mimic it is within us all.

Water gardening as a style is very old, and its potential has been appreciated since Classical

Fig 6 A pond, whether large or small, should be considered as part of the total garden layout.

times. The Romans, great garden builders, brought the ideas of the Mediterranean to the lands which they conquered, and made, amongst other features, lead ponds. With their departure these lands once more reverted to savagery; gardening, along with virtually all aspects of culture, disappeared and with it the man-made water gardens. The monasteries in part provided the revival of interest in water – the monks saw it only in an agricultural sense, for farming the carp that were so important to their diet. The ideas for water gardening as we know it today were almost certainly imported from Renaissance Europe. In the late sixteenth century Sir Francis Bacon designed a most ambitious water garden, which, although never built, does show that the principle was accepted, if not yet established in the UK. In the next two centuries elaborate water gardens were to be constructed in the vast estates of

Fig 7   *A gazebo provides both a scenic background, and will also function as a shed or storage room for tools.*

the wealthy. The creation of water gardens and ponds in the gardens of the suburbs dates from about the 1930s. Up until this time their establishment and maintenance was viewed with trepidation, and they were often considered beyond the ability of all but the best professional gardeners.

It was also a long-held belief (and one that is still maintained by some people) that only a large garden could have a pond. On the contrary, ponds can be included in any size of plot. Where there is room for a flower bed there is room for a water garden. However, such a garden must be designed with water in mind and the other features must fit around it. Ponds may make up the total garden, may be a central feature of a larger scheme or may be effectively separated from the rest of the plot. All sizes and shapes can be accommodated, and any thoughts of failure can be dismissed, providing that the creator studies and understands the

subject rather than rushing out, spade in hand, to dig a hole. For example, if fish are to be kept, it is necessary to appreciate the amount of room that they require and to resist the temptation to over-stock the pool.

Water is at its most effective where it will bring out the best in other garden features, and where they in turn will make the most of the water. Water fits into every type of design, from the classical or formal styles, to the geometric designs of the patio-style garden and the decorated approach, in which statuettes, windmills and other man-made features are included to complete the scene. If good water gardening is one of the finest features of a garden, nothing is quite as bad as water poorly used. The use of water must be very carefully planned, for whilst it is usually possible to fit water into every type of garden, this does not mean that water can be included at any position. A small pond fitted in to a rock garden almost as though it were an additional plant providing a type of groundcover does not work. Water and rocks, with their ageless character, go well together, and the best designs for a water garden incorporate the use of rocks, but the balance of the two features is very important. They must appear to live in harmony, with neither dominating the other.

Modern pond moulds and pond liners are excellent, involving less work, expense and skill to site than the older concrete ponds, but where their presence is seen the whole effect is destroyed. A water garden should either appear to be· a perfectly natural part of the environment or clearly a man-made creation, but in either case there is no place for intrusive modern plastics. The other disappointing effect to avoid is a green, slime-like growth covering the surface of the pond, where microscopic forms of life, carried on the wind or the feet of visiting birds, colonise the pond. The balance of the organic aspect – life – is just as important as

Fig 8   (Opposite) *A pond carefully sited in a woodland setting.*

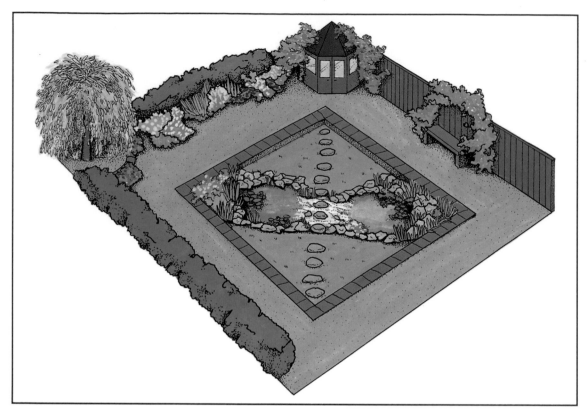

Fig 9   The water garden should be planned in terms of the garden as a whole, and a plan drawn up before any work is attempted.

the inorganic – the rocks and materials which make up the structure. A balanced environment, which is not difficult to create, will ensure that there are predators to feed off the microscopic forms of life which cause the problems in the water garden.

So, water gardening has the potential to create beauty and provide satisfaction, and yet requires the minimum amount of attention and expense. Moreover, once created, a pond is there for life; there is no need to redesign it as with a flower bed, because it will never be static. However, success is only possible if the garden is carefully planned and designed, and the skills are fully understood. Anyone can include a pond or water garden within their design, whether they possess a large garden or a small one, and this book will explain in simple terms how to plan it, build it and maintain it without trouble.

WORDS OF CAUTION

Water can be dangerous, and this should never be overlooked. Even the most shallow pond is deep enough to drown someone, especially a small child, and a fascinating water garden should never be constructed where unsupervised children are liable to play. Water and electricity are a lethal combination and not for the enthusiastic 'do-it-yourselfer'. If you are thinking of including electrics in your layout, leave it to a fully qualified electrician. Ponds can be constructed as part of a roof garden, but this should definitely be avoided by the amateur. Water is extremely heavy, and this puts a tremendous strain on the roof. Unless the pond is correctly constructed, the water could come bursting through. Should you contemplate such an approach, employ a competent professional with adequate insurance!

CHAPTER 1

Siting the Water Garden

The most important consideration, which must be correctly resolved before any construction work is attempted, is the position of your proposed water garden. Although the water garden has its own special demands, it must be planned in terms of the garden as a whole. The garden layout you choose will dictate the position, and, to some extent, the shape and size of the pool, and the water feature must harmonise with the overall scheme in all respects. Should you choose to make water the central theme of your garden, or of a part of the garden which is separated by a screen or other visual obstruction, the whole area must be

Fig 10   The water garden is an essential feature of the larger plot.

Fig 11   *When planning a water garden it is advisable to work out the advantages of the various sites on paper first.*

designed in such a way that an aesthetic balance is created.

The water garden must have adequate sunlight. This is needed to penetrate the water and allow the water weeds to perform photosynthesis in order to maintain the dissolved oxygen level in the water. Green algae is sometimes said to grow as a result of a pond receiving too much sunlight, but this is not correct, for it thrives where there is an excess of nutrients and an absence of predators to live off it. It is, therefore, the result of a poor environmental balance. The water garden should also be protected as far as possible from the worst effects of easterly and westerly winds, otherwise the plants may become damaged or broken, or at the very least suffer from wind burn, where the extremities of the leaves turn brown, then black, before falling off.

The factors affecting the siting of a water garden are the same whether it is to be a new feature in an established garden, or the whole garden is being designed for the first time. Before embarking on any plan you must study the climatic conditions and see how they affect your garden; ignoring this could result in expensive failure. However, ponds do not require perfect conditions and pampering, and there is a degree of latitude on most sites that allows for a choice of positions.

Fig 12   A pond may be constructed in a wooded area and where there are hedges providing that shadows are not thrown over the pond for any length of time during the day and that leaves are not allowed to enter the water.

In narrowing down the possible sites for your water garden, first omit all the areas where it is impractical to build the feature, such as a front open-plan garden which may be liable to damage by dogs, or areas which are hidden from view. Next, draw a scale plan of the whole, marking the areas which are in shade and which should be avoided. The length of shadow that any object will throw should be appreciated. It may not be possible to find a position which is totally free of all shadows, but you should look for the position which enjoys the maximum amount of daily sunlight. In this respect the effect of trees should also be carefully considered, for apart from the problems of the leaves falling they may throw a shadow across part or all of the pond. Next, establish the true north of the garden, mark it clearly on the diagram and include the directions of the prevailing winds. The intensity of the winds will depend very much on the position of the garden. If you are situated in an exposed location, near to the sea or on the side of a steep hill, you will suffer far stronger effects of wind than if you are in a valley. Valleys will often act as frost traps, but this slight difference in temperature is unlikely to be sufficient to cause problems. Every area has microclimates which may be considerably different from the larger area as a whole. There will also be degrees of microclimate – a county on the western seaboard will have a far wetter climate than the rest of the country, while coasts washed by the gulf stream will have a warmer climate than would be expected for the latitude. Consequently, those towns nearer the water will usually be at higher temperatures than landlocked towns in the same county. Within the town itself there will be different climatic conditions, depending upon the degree of exposure or the nearness to buildings which may be emitting their own heat. Within the garden itself there will be hot spots (such as against a south-facing wall), while exposed positions may be vulnerable to frosts, receiving them earlier in the year, and of a greater intensity in winter.

ELEVATIONS

With all but the simplest planting schemes there will be differences in height, and, looking across the garden from the main vantage point, the furthermost part will be elevated compared with the flat level of the pond. Such high levels should ideally be at the northern boundary of the plot having a southerly aspect, but plots are seldom constructed with a simple north – south elevation, and tend to lie between the cardinal points of the compass. Where it is impossible to obtain an exactly south-facing site it is best either to get as near to a southerly aspect as possible, or to use the easterly aspect (where it will be necessary to give careful consideration to the effects of the wind). The soil itself takes a large amount of heat from the atmosphere to warm up just a few degrees, and is also a poor conductor of heat. As a consequence of the high heat capacity, the deeper you go into the ground the less the temperature changes as a result of the seasons, and heat (or lack of it) at the earth's surface. This is particularly important to the pond builder, because at the bottom of a deepish pond there will be water that is less susceptible to change. Although it will slowly rise to the surface by convection currents and be subjected to the heat losses at this point, it effectively stops the water from freezing completely, except in the severest winters. The water can freeze solid when ponds are built above ground level. In certain protected areas in the south of England, or where there is a favourable microclimate, such ponds will present no problems in most years, but during the very severe winters that occur from time to time, the possibility of the water freezing solid with the total loss of the animate pond life, cannot be ruled out.

Where wind is a particular problem it will be necessary to construct a windbreak. Walls and solid fences effectively provide protection to a distance of about three times their height from the wall itself. At midday, when the sun is at its most intense, the length of the shadow will be

Fig 13 *The small water garden with running water may be situated on most sites. It has a charm and beauty all of its own.*

equal to the height of the wall, so clearly there is an area which will receive a maximum amount of sunlight and which will still be afforded protection from the wind. A hedge is a better windbreak than a solid wall, which only deflects the wind to some other position. A hedge, fence, or screen in which there are gaps, breaks up the air current, offering the maximum protection while not concentrating the air to form a strong draught. Moreover, a hedge often blends into the overall garden design far better than a wall.

SIZE

In some gardens the size of the area which can be given over to the water garden will be restricted, but even in modern high-density estate developments there is always room to construct a whole water garden with marginals and bogs. Where there is a restriction on size, it is better to build a larger pond and to omit the bog garden, and even if necessary reduce the margins, rather than try to get too much into a confined space. The smallest practical size for a pond is about 6ft (180cm) by 4ft (120cm). It *is* possible to construct smaller ponds, and they can give you much pleasure for raising plants, keeping fish and attracting wildlife, but at that size they are not a landscape feature and are better thought of as outdoor aquariums. The larger the pond the fewer problems it will create and the wider the range of wildlife it will attract. Ponds require a depth of at least 2ft (60cm); this extra depth is needed not only for water-lilies to grow, but to accommodate the fish during cold winter spells, and to reduce the likelihood of the pond freezing solid. Regardless of the surface area, always ensure that you have this depth of water. (An outdoor aquarium is an exception to this rule, which need not apply if you intend only to grow miniature water-lilies. However, the reduced size may restrict the growth of any goldfish that you may wish to include.)

A small water garden should not be thought of in terms of miniaturisation of a large aquascape, but rather as an individual design, tailor-made for the space that is available.

THE GARDEN PLAN

Having decided the possible sites from a climatic point of view and the limitations imposed by the size of the plot, you need to decide which of the suitable positions (there will almost certainly be more than one), is the best in terms of the overall garden design. You could plan your overall garden design, with the water garden provisionally 'pencilled in', and then decide whether there are any problems in terms of climate, and whether you could resolve them by the use of windbreaks or other appropriate structures. Whichever approach you use, it is important that the water garden is seen as part of the whole and its broader role in the garden design is appreciated from the outset. Never start building the water garden or any part of the garden until you have fully planned the whole plot. Decide the theme of your garden and then design the water garden accordingly. There are six main styles of garden.

The Formal Garden

The formal garden is based on symmetry, and the elements that make it up have straight, sharp edges with rigid right angles. They may alternatively be designed based on a circle or oval if the overall plan demands it. Total harmony will exist between all of the features: there will be well-tended beds, laid out in geometrical patterns, and immaculate lawns with sharp edges. Think very carefully before incorporating any more than a pond in such a design as, although a margin will not necessarily appear irregular, many of the marginal plants are not of a type to blend in with a fully formal garden design. Moreover, the flowers will tend to be overshadowed by those in the borders or by the roses (a popular feature of formal gardens), both of which are dominant in their impact. Ponds for formal gardens will normally be of a rectangular or square shape, reflecting the shape of the garden as a whole, and flagstones are laid at the edge for the sharp angles that are the important feature. Where formal gardens are based on the use of curves and arcs, round or oval-shaped ponds are constructed to mimic the overall shape.

The pond should be situated at the centre of the plot to produce a perfectly balanced overall design – a formal garden always has a centre or plane of symmetry which acts as a focal point. Water-lilies, with their bold, almost rose-like global flowers, are the only plants that blend totally into the formal system. Because of the harmony that exists between the water-lily and the rose, rose gardens, which are usually constructed as a special type of formal garden, are particularly suited to the inclusion of a regularly-shaped pond as a centrepiece. Where water-lilies are used in a formal setting they should be replanted from time to time to ensure that no more than one-third of the surface area of

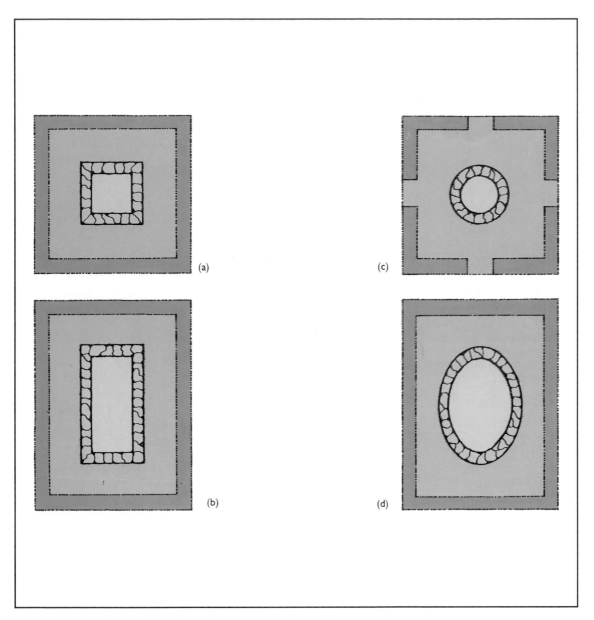

Fig 14   Layout of ponds into a formal garden. (a) Totally formal but
nevertheless a style which is always in fashion – the square pond inside the
square plot; (b) with a rectangular plot the pond should be of the same
proportions as the plot itself; (c) the pure curves of the circle alone are
capable of balancing the sharp angles and equal sides of the square; (d) an
oval pond with the proportion of the maximum to minimum axes the same as
that of the side of the plot. **Note:** You should never place a rectangular pond
in a square garden or vice versa; never place an oval or rectangular shape
contrary to the direction of the plot; in a formal garden the pond must
harmonise with the plot.

Fig 15   A formal fountain and pool.

water is covered with the floating leaves. (It
may be necessary to allow an increase in coverage if algae growth is a problem.) The irregular
growth of irises should also be avoided. Formal
gardens are not intended to appear natural, but
are an art form in which the gardener is always
in complete command.

The plan of the garden will dictate the position of the pond. Formal gardens demand an
open, sunny aspect, to show off to the best
advantage the bright colours and design features. The only visible pond plants will be the
water-hugging lilies, and they will be less prone
to wind damage than higher-growing subjects
would. It may be assumed that any location that
is suitable for a formal garden may successfully
accommodate a pond.

Fig 16   (Right) A clump of water-lilies at the
centre of a crucifix. Bright colours may be
maintained throughout the year by container-
grown plants.

The Informal Garden

Paradoxically, the informal garden is also completely planned, and always under the control of its creator. The effect is intended, however, to be more 'natural', with the lines being softer, to give the impression that nature is in command. Such gardens allow for more latitude, and it is here that the complete water garden can be created. The initial impression is one of the shapes and details created by the vegetation, and water and rocks are natural subjects for inclusion into such scenes. There are two main types of informal garden in which water may be included, the cottage garden and the rock garden.

The Cottage Garden

This often looks simply like a disoriented patch in which old-fashioned flowers are grown, but in fact it also requires planning around a simple theme. There are usually herbaceous or mixed beds containing a variety of shrubs, annuals and perennials, and the casual, apparently carefree effect belies the meticulous attention to detail which has gone into their creation. In such gardens water may be the main theme, passing through all depths until all that remain are the dry plant beds. Alternatively, if climatic factors demand, the water garden may be situated at one of the sides or, if the aspect dictates, in one of the corners. The demands of the water

Fig 17 Marginal planting.

garden may be allowed to take precedence over all others, and this type of design encourages the inclusion of all shapes and shades of plant growth, and the greatest variety of pond marginals and bog plants.

The principle of planning terrestrial beds is well understood, and the same rules can be applied to water garden designs. Such a feature is seldom studied at short range, but more frequently viewed from a distance, and the observer should be able to take in all the organic and inorganic characteristics with a sweep of his eyes. When preparing your plan you need to decide the point from which you wish to observe the water garden, perhaps from a window in the house (the British weather means that more time is spent looking out on to the garden than in the garden itself). If the garden fronts on to the street, you may wish to create the garden so that the passer-by derives the maximum benefit. It is possible to design a garden where the view is virtually the same from the house and the street, more so with the formal symmetrical pond than with the informal system, because in the latter the taller subjects need to be placed to the back of the pond. One of the commonest faults in many water gardens with a good selection of mar-

Fig 18   A natural-looking waterfall.

Fig 19 *A watercourse amongst a rockery with stones of the district remains one of the most difficult layouts to improve upon.*

ginals and bog plants is that taller subjects, such as irises, are at the front of the pond, obscuring the rest of the plants from view.

The planting scheme for all the plants involved will need to be plotted out on a plan of the water garden, with the largest subjects at the back, and the small upright plants progressively further and further to the front. Water-

lilies, with their low-growing habit, will perform a role similar to that of the pansy in the herbaceous bed. Either all the taller-growing subjects can be to the back, or there may be a gradual lessening of height along the side, with an empty open area at the front of the pond, so that the water-lilies may be seen from the original designated vantage point.

Due regard must be given to the position of the garden relative to the points of the compass. For example, if the pond is on the south side of the property because of the restrictions imposed by the vantage point, then the tall subjects cannot be planted at the back. Instead, the water needs an open aspect down the centre of its concourse, in order that the water-lilies receive the maximum amount of sunlight. Plant the pond and marginals down the sides, but retain the principle of the tallest being furthest away from the observer.

The Rock Garden

Water and stone both have great age, and together they produce an eternal effect to give a sense of timelessness to a garden. Virtually all ponds have some stone or concrete associated with them. In the rock garden pond, part of the land surrounding the water is raised and used to construct a rock or alpine garden. In many senses the rock garden which needs a high level of drainage to grow alpines – which draw the water they need from the thin film of moisture adhering by surface tension to the underside of the stones – is the reverse of a water garden. However, they do work well together if you carefully select the alpine subjects which survive most conditions, providing their roots are dry. By combining both a rock and water garden it is possible to achieve one of the most natural looking of landscapes, but although the two blend together from a horticultural point of view, it is best to consider the rock garden and the pool as separate entities.

There is another important advantage to including a rock garden with a pond: constructing the pond will produce a great deal of spoilage in the form of top soil, and large amounts of work, and the problems associated with redepositing it, can be avoided by using it to create a rockery to the rear of the pool. This will give the garden more than one level, with plant height ranging from the floating lily pads to the highest alpine. Concentrated into the small space of a modern garden, all this will give the area a sense of mass.

So there are very strong arguments for creating a rock garden in conjunction with a water garden. If this approach appeals to you, not only should the whole garden be designed before any work is attempted, but also the fine detail should be worked out, such as the quantity of rock required. Order all at the same time, so that even if it is not possible to do all of the work at once, the rock will match throughout. It may also be cheaper to buy a single load of stone, which will involve just one journey from the quarry.

Classical Gardens

Within a relatively small plot (but perhaps not in a really tiny modern estate garden) it is possible to create a classical style garden, which takes its inspiration from the seventeenth and eighteenth century landscaped designs. Here the emphasis is not on bright colours – virtually all of the visual effect is created by green, including all shades, from the dark green of privet, through the medium green of a lawn, to the almost yellow-green of certain cultivars or shrubs. The main harmonising colour is the grey white of limestone which makes up the pond. Bright-coloured flowers are used extremely cautiously, but include daffodils in spring, summer favourites, such as antirrhinum, and Michaelmas daisies for the autumn. The eye is instinctively drawn towards these and care must be taken to ensure that they do not predominate and take over the scene. The garden depends very much upon the form of the trees and shrubs (their height, mass and shape) creating a living organic sculpture, a constantly changing scene. The pondscape and structure provide the only element that is not dependent upon the seasons of the year.

There is a degree of latitude in the shaping of the pond, which may be either round, or of an unsymmetrical shape. The important factor is to use stone which has aged since it was cut and

Fig 20   Here are all the elements that make for the classic water garden –
aged stone, water plants and a backcloth of greenery. The bench allows the
observer to sit mesmerised by the moving water.

dressed to give a totally natural appearance.
You may find such stone on a demolition site,
and it will be well worth rescuing and cheaper
than the fresh-cut material. Accessories, in the
form of reproduction classical sculptures or
fountains, may be included in the design. Do
ensure, however, that they are made of a
material that will blend with that of the pond
surrounds. Do not spoil the effect by using
obviously cheap and inferior plastic models.

Ornamental Gardens

In an ornamental garden a large number of
accessories are used to give a certain feel to the
plot. Such gardens cover an enormous range,
from baroque or even rococo, to the ubiquitous garden gnomes, but whatever your
taste water will almost certainly find its way in.
The pond, which can be of any shape, may be
kept relatively simple. The plants are secondary

Fig 21 Ornaments for the water garden. (a) A well-built wishing well is an asset in any garden; (b) cast iron, once so popular with the Victorians, is enjoying a revival; (c) not to everyone's taste, but to their fans garden gnomes are a must for any garden.

to the artefacts and little beyond water-lilies need be grown. Marginals will represent a further complication, tending to detract from the inorganics. The pond and rocks may be the only permanent features in an area which will change with the whim of fashion – windmills, bridges and similar features will allow the creator to display his woodworking skills.

The Patio

The origins of patio gardening are very old indeed, and the name is derived from the Spanish for 'courtyard'. It is only in recent years that the approach has become very popular with urban gardeners, and a sizeable part of the fast-growing garden centre trade has been directed towards the patio gardener. With its less demanding calls on space and the time of the owner, patio gardening is tailor-made for the modern life-style. Perhaps more than any other type of garden, a patio demands the use of water, to provide necessary variety in a visual sense to break up the stonework. However, the styles of water garden that are appropriate are strictly limited. In general the

Fig 22　A totally modern approach in this pond is set amongst paving stones and patio slabs.

Fig 23　The basic design for the inclusion of a pond system within a patio.

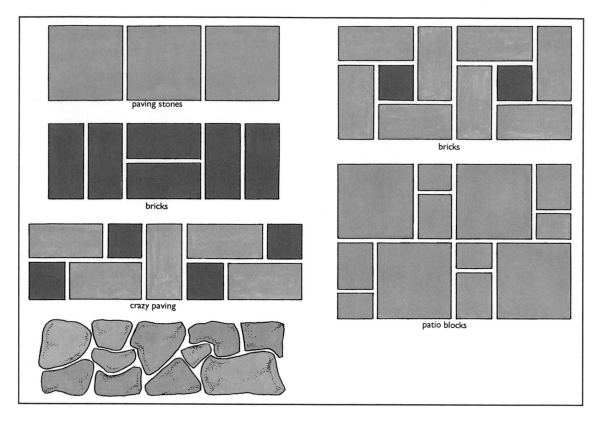

paving stones

bricks

bricks

crazy paving

patio blocks

Fig 24   Examples of simple and complex surrounds.

patio lends itself to a geometrical, usually rectangular type of pool (most conveniently constructed from either liners or fibreglass moulds). Using concrete it is possible to make two modest pools, interconnected with 4in (10cm) pipe. Alternatively, an overlap of 4in (10cm) of the patio slabs may be provided, where the fish will shelter. Where the patio itself is constructed on two levels a waterfall may be included, with the water cascading from the upper level. The visual effect, together with the sound, will accentuate the differences in height. Each pool may be made to suit different types of water-lily, but generally a shallower structure is favourable. No fountain should produce a jet of more than about 24in (60cm). It is important to keep everything in proportion in the small courtyard-type layout.

Within all garden designs there will be a natural place for water, but in including this element you must ensure that it harmonises, reflecting the features of the other parts of the design. Remember always that the design must be very carefully considered – it is far easier to move features around on paper than it is to manhandle soils and rocks. To get a better idea of the visual effect of the water garden, mark out the shape of the pond in the position that it is to occupy with 3ft (1m) rods. Examine the result from all positions, including, importantly, from your most likely vantage point in the house, considering the view of your garden which you will most frequently see. Change the position of the rods until you are completely satisfied with the effect, then permanently mark out the area to be occupied by the pond.

CHAPTER 2

Building the Pond

Natural ponds do occur in some gardens but they are relatively rare, usually in association with a layer of clay near to the surface. This layer effectively stops the water from escaping and, providing that it acts as part of a natural drainage system and sufficient rainfall is received, it will maintain a relatively constant level, creating what is perhaps the best pond of all. Apart from construction, natural ponds may be considered similar in every way to the man-made equivalent. In order to create movement a second, artificial pond, above the level of the natural one, may be created.

In the vast majority of instances, however, there will be no natural pond, and the gardener will have to construct one. There are three basic ways of doing this – with concrete, with a liner, or with a fibreglass mould.

Fig 25   This is a formally designed but irregularly-shaped pool with a fountain.

THE CONCRETE POND

In many respects concrete is the best material to use for making ponds, and for many years was the only one available. Today it is the most expensive, and for even the smallest pond considerably more physical work in terms of moving and mixing cement and sand is involved than with other methods – where even a modest size of pond is contemplated it may well pay to hire a small cement mixer. The cost is the major disadvantage of the method. Thick, strong sides to the pond are necessary to withstand the forces created and the effects of freezing, and a 4in (10cm) concrete wall is the thinnest which can be relied upon to perform the task. If you are considering using concrete it is advisable to calculate the quantity and cost of materials at the outset.

Dimensions

Rectangular Ponds

In imperial units   To build a pond 4in (⅓ft) thick. Take all the following measurements in feet. W=width, D=depth, B=breadth. The addition is made to include the volume necessary to create the floor of the pond. The result will be in cubic feet – to convert to cubic yards, divide by 27.

$$([2W \times D] + [2B \times D]) \times 1/3 + (W \times B \times 1/3)$$

Where the pond is to be of varying depths, such as where a shelf is to be constructed for marginals, the calculation must be modified to take this into account. The effect of the step will be equivalent to the shortfall, produced as a lack of depth at the shallow end, and the calculation in respect of the breadth will remain the same for both ends. The difference will occur in the sides, which should each be considered as two components, made up of two distinct lengths and depths. Should you wish to create the pond at three distinct levels (which

might be necessary if you intend to grow a range of plants which require different water depths), you will need to perform the calculation employing three distinct components for this item.

Example   The amount of concrete needed to build a rectangular pond 9ft by 6ft, to a depth of 2ft for two-thirds of the length and a depth of 6in for the remaining third, the whole to be made from 4in concrete.

$2 \times 6 \times 2 = 24$ sq ft (6ft being the length of the deepest part of the pond)

$2 \times 3 \times 1/2 = 3$ sq ft (3ft being the length of the shallower part of the pond)

$2 \times 6 \times 2 = 24$ sq ft (this is the side at the deep end)

The total area is 51 sq ft

The base is $6 \times 9 = 54$ sq ft

The total area is 105 sq ft

The total volume is $105 \times 1/3 = 35$ cu ft

27 cu ft in a cu yd, therefore the amount of concrete required is 35 divided by 27 = approx. **1 1/3 cu yds**

So, to build such a pond you would need 1 1/3 cu yds of concrete.

In metric units   Metric volumes are all expressed in cubic metres. Measure everything in metres and express the measurements as a whole number of metres plus the decimal part of the metre; for example, 10cm is 0.1m, and 60cm is 0.6m. Multiply the total area by 0.1m (10cm) to find the volume of cement required – the extra is necessary to provide a wall of 10cm thickness. W = width, D = depth, B = breadth.

Example   To build a pond similar to the one described above, the calculations are as follows:

$2 \times 2 \times 0.6 = 2.4$ sq m

Circular Ponds

The area of the side of a circular pond will be found by multiplying the diameter by 2 then by π (22/7 or 3.142). The base is given by π times the radius squared.

On a pond of 6ft diameter, the boundary length will be 6 × 22/7 = 132/7 = 19 sq ft (approx.)

If the pond is uniformly 2ft deep then the area of the wall is 38 sq ft

The base is 3 × 3 × 22/7 = 198/7 = 28 sq ft (approx.)

The total area is 28 + 38 sq ft = 66 sq ft

The volume of concrete required for a thickness of 4in is 66/3 = 22/27 cu yd (approx.)

If a shelf 6in deep is included, the total surface area to be covered with concrete is reduced by 1ft. This amount is insignificant and may be ignored for the purposes of calculation.

In metric units, a similar pond would be 2m in diameter, with a depth of 60cm.

The surface area of the side is 2 × 3.142 × 0.6 = 3.76 sq m

The surface area of the base is 3.142 × 1 = 3.142 sq m

The total surface area is 3.76 + 3.142 = 6.9 sq m

The total volume required for a thickness of 10cm = 0.69 cu m

Oval Ponds

The mathematics required to calculate the quantity of concrete for an oval pond are very complex. The best is to obtain an approximate value by assuming the minor and major axes are the sides of a rectangle, and calculate as for

Fig 26 *A beautiful display of flowers surrounds this concrete pool.*

2 × 1 × 0.15 = 0.3 sq m

2 × 2 × 0.6 = 2.4 sq m

The total area of the sides of the pond = 5.1 sq m

The area of the base is 3 × 2 = 6 sq m

The total area is 6 + 5.1 = 11.1

The volume of concrete required to build such a pond to a thickness of 10cm is 11.1 × 0.1 = **1.11 cu m**

of the string is multiplied by the depth and the thickness of the concrete to give the volume necessary for the pond wall. This volume, together with that of the base, is the total amount of concrete required.

Irregular-shaped Ponds

For irregular ponds, use the grid method described above for working out the area of an oval pond.

Building the Concrete Pond

Ponds should not be built during the worst parts of the winter when drainage can present a problem, moreover concrete should not be laid during frosty weather as it will not set correctly and will lack structural strength, making it more vulnerable to cracking. Pond building can involve a great deal of physical work and require the movement of large quantities of top soil, so before any work is attempted you should plan where the soil is to be placed. Bear in mind that the soil, especially if it is good quality loam, may be used for a raised structure such as a rock garden. When moving soil, take the top fertile layer away and place to one side before moving any of the subsoil which lacks the humus to maintain plant life. Ensure that the fertile layer is returned to the top of any structure built with the excavated earth. Often ponds are constructed in lawns in which it is intended to retain the lawn after the water garden has been constructed. To protect the lawn, cover the area where any sub-soil is to be deposited with a tarpaulin or even heavy-duty plastic sheeting, avoiding materials that tear easily as it may be subjected to rough treatment. Transporting rocks to the site and soil away from it will usually require a wheelbarrow, and the heavy weight on the wheel can result in a ridge being cut in the lawn. Avoid this problem by placing planks on the lawn to form a track over which the barrow may be pushed.

Decide the size of the pond that you require

Fig 27   *Here container-grown greenery provides an attractive complement for a pool in a woodland setting.*

a rectangular pond. This will give you a greater volume of concrete than you actually need.

For a more accurate estimate, mark out a grid divided into 12in squares, and draw the oval on to the grid. Count the squares covered by the oval, and then add up the fractions of the squares that are not completely covered. This should give you a reasonably accurate estimate of the area involved. Multiply the area by 4in (1/3ft) to give the volume of cement required in cubic feet.

The boundary of such a pond is best found by marking out the site and using a piece of string to define the circumference. The length

Fig 28   Pond shapes in addition to the simple single geometrical design.

then construct a hole 4in (10cm) deeper at all points – including any shelfing – and 8in (20cm) longer and wider to allow for the volume occupied by the cement. When the hole has been dug, construct shuttering all around the sides at a distance of 4in (10cm) from the side. The shuttering may be built from spare timber that you possess, providing it is ½ – 1in (1 – 3cm) thick. Wood suitable for this purpose can be found on a demolition site in the form of old floor boards or similar material. Hold the shuttering in place by means of 2 x 2in (5 x 5cm) stakes or similar. Before applying the cement thoroughly soak the shuttering. When it dries cement contracts, and the amount of the shrinkage will depend upon how wet the mixture was originally. If the boards are well soaked the mixture will be very wet in the region of the wood, causing extra shrinkage and the dried concrete will readily come away from the shuttering. To reinforce the concrete, place a piece of 1in mesh chicken wire in the middle of the space to be filled with concrete. Pour in the concrete, taking care that it is distributed on either side of the chicken wire. Allow the cement to dry out completely, then carefully remove the shuttering.

Next, lay the floor of the pond. This is a relatively simple task. Place a layer of about 2in (5cm) of concrete at the bottom of the excavated hole, put the reinforcing chicken wire into position and cover with the second 2in (5cm) of concrete. Use a builder's float and check with a spirit level to ensure that the surface is flat. With small ponds vertical sides are the only practical way of maximising the deep water

33

thickness may be used in the construction. Where ponds are built with a slope, calculations of quantities must be adjusted accordingly. The construction is best accomplished by planning the depth that you intend the pond to have, which may be 'zero' depth at the edge to 24in (60cm) at the centre. Allow an additional 4in (10cm) (for the thickness of cement) at all positions. Having marked out the area, drive in a number of rods to the required depth, then excavate the hole using the rods for guidance. There will be no need for shuttering. The floor is constructed in a similar fashion to the flat-bottomed pond, using the float to obtain a smooth surface. Do not worry if the angle of the bottom is not perfect, as you will not notice it when the pond is covered in lilies. Moreover, the water itself tends to distort the view through it, the depth appearing as only three-quarters of its true value.

With any method of construction using cement it is imperative that you do not leave a join at the position where the sides meet the floor – contraction of the cement will leave a gap. If a gap does result, further cement must be forced into the position or (preferably) one of the sealing compounds designed for repairing leaky ponds. Such systems are not always totally effective, so it is better to make sure that there are no gaps in the first place. With a concrete pond the containing areas for the marginals may be constructed with blocks at the same time as the pond itself is built.

Cement is made by heating together clay and chalk to a very high temperature, and as a result of this operation some free lime is formed which will dissolve into the water and raise the pH. This will be harmful to both the fish and the plant life. Fortunately, lime is very soluble and it may be removed by filling the pond with water and letting it stand for a day, draining, then repeating the process a further five times. This will give you water of the correct pH, but it is wasteful and time consuming. A more practical solution is to cover the concrete surfaces of the pond with 'Silglaze', which is a sealant designed

Fig 29 *Careful choice of shape is extremely important in terms of the design of the garden as a whole.*

area. The side of a pond is effectively a retaining wall and it must, therefore, possess sufficient thickness to provide the necessary mechanical strength.

Building a wall with a slope allows for the construction of a thinner wall, and with the shallowest slopes cement of half the normal

Fig 30   Section through a pond showing the walls with at least 15° batters to increase their strength. The marginals are planted in troughs created by a brickwork structure, whilst the water-lilies are planted in purpose-built containers.

specifically for the purpose. It should be applied according to the manufacturer's instructions.

POND LINERS

Using pond liners represents the most versatile of the methods of pond construction, providing a barrier or membrane between the soil and the water. The shape of the pond is first excavated, then a layer of plastic sheeting is placed into the hole, which is filled with water. Providing that the plastic does not break, the pond will be a permanent structure. The success of the method depends not only on the method of construction but on the nature of the material from which the liner is made. All the different materials that are available are plastics made from products obtained mainly from crude petroleum. Several molecules of the starting material are joined together to form the plastic; the individual properties of the plastics will depend upon that starting material, and may vary quite considerably in spite of the names appearing to be similar. Some plastics carry the prefix 'poly', denoting that several molecules are involved, whereas others do not, but the process of manufacture of all of them, is similar.

The name 'plastic' means pliable and, although many of the petroleum-based materials are only mouldable at high temperatures, some do retain a degree of elasticity at ambient temperature. This is essential when the pond is being filled with water, to ensure that any slight stretching as a result of uneven water pressure does not permanently damage the membrane.

The main plastics used for pond liners are:

Butyl rubber   This is the most widely used of the pond lining materials and may be safely recommended for use in all water garden constructions.

Polyvinylchloride (PVC)   This is a plastic material that is used extensively in horticulture. The thicker sheets are a useful material for pond construction.

Plastolene   This effectively overcomes the main problem associated with PVC sheeting (which is reduced mechanical strength), by reinforcing with a matrix of another plastic.

Fig 31 Making a garden pond with a liner. (a) Excavate the pond to your chosen shape; (b) check with a spirit level that the bottom is level, and also look to see that there are no sharp flints or other materials that could cut the liner; (c) place the liner over the hole, allowing sufficient plastic to take up the shape of the hole; Hold in position by means of pieces of rock or crazy paving; (d) allow the water to trickle in through the hose, releasing the rocks from time to time to avoid unnecessary stretching of the liner; (e) once the pond is filled to within 2in (5cm) of the top, remove the hose and completely obscure the liner with the crazy paving.

The Size of the Sheeting

You will need a piece of sheeting that covers the area of the pond, plus both the length and the breadth increased by twice the depth, together with a further 3ft (1m) to provide an 18in (50cm) overlay around the pond.

For a rectangular pond 9ft by 6ft and 2ft deep, the length required is:

$9 + 2 + 2 + 1\frac{1}{2} + 1\frac{1}{2} = 16$ft

(The metric equivalent is $3 + 0.6 + 0.6 + 0.45 + 0.45 = 5.1$m)

The breadth required is:

$6 + 2 + 2 + 1\frac{1}{2} + 1\frac{1}{2} = 13$ft

(The metric equivalent is $2 + 0.6 + 0.6 + 0.45 + 0.45 = 4.1$m)

No reduction can be made at this stage for the shelf for marginals. The extra overlap should simply be cut away.

If you intend to include a bog garden in the scheme, add on the area in square feet that you wish to include, either to the length or the breadth, whichever is the most appropriate. For an irregular shaped pond the largest width and breadth must be taken, and the whole treated as though it were a rectangular pond, with the excess being trimmed away.

Constructing the Pond

Mark out the sides of the area to be excavated on the ground and dig out the size of the hole required. There will be no need to remove a larger area (as in the case of the concrete pond), as the volume occupied by the plastic sheeting is negligible. You must ensure that the base is firm, as subsidence will almost certainly result in stress in the liner, which could make it susceptible to damage at that point. If there is any likelihood of this occurring, dig down to a firm base and fill back up to the correct depth with sand. Check with a spirit level that the base is flat. Once the hole has been excavated make sure that there are no sharp stones or gravel which could puncture the sheeting. Remember that stresses will be set up in the plastic sheeting whilst it is being filled with water, when it is more liable to rupture. Although repairs are possible, they present complications, and are far better avoided by careful forethought. If there is a large quantity of gravel or other subsoil which could present problems, cover the surface with sand. Sides are far more difficult and the greatest care must be taken to avoid the occurrence of any jagged edges.

Outside the area covered by the pond remove top soil to a depth of 3in (7.5cm) to allow for the overlap. Place quality turves to one side for replacement once the operation is complete. If you are constructing a bog garden, excavate the additional area to a depth of 6in (15cm). Lay the sheeting inside the pond and place the edges exactly 18in (45cm) from the sides of the hole.

To fill with water temporarily secure the plastic in place by means of heavy planks, bricks or rockery stones, or any other sufficiently heavy material which can readily be removed for repositioning of the sheeting during the filling process. Place the hose pipe in the pond and let the water in at first at a trickle. Do not be impatient or try to speed the process up at this stage. Keep a sharp look-out for any strain occurring, any unevenness in the flooring, or any depressions forming as a result of the weight of the water – the sheeting will stretch and a point of weakness will be created. If any strains do occur, release the weights holding the plastic in position, and you should be able to rearrange the plastic slightly to overcome the problem, if the area under stress is not too large. When the pond has filled with water, secure the sheet in position by placing the turves or rocks in their permanent position. Do not be tempted to cement the stones in position. Carefully select them so that the gaps between them are as small and as regular as possible.

Fig 32   Fibreglass pools are available in various shapes and sizes.

FIBREGLASS PONDS

Fibreglass is a material consisting of a plastic resin reinforced with strands of glass, which is readily moulded into a whole range of different shapes and sizes, including precast pond moulds. These pond moulds are sometimes shunned by garden purists as being restrictive in both shape and size, however, they are really a modern product designed for today's market, satisfying the needs of the owners of smaller gardens. As such, they are the most suitable choice for a variety of locations. Fibreglass liners do tend to be expensive compared with pond

38

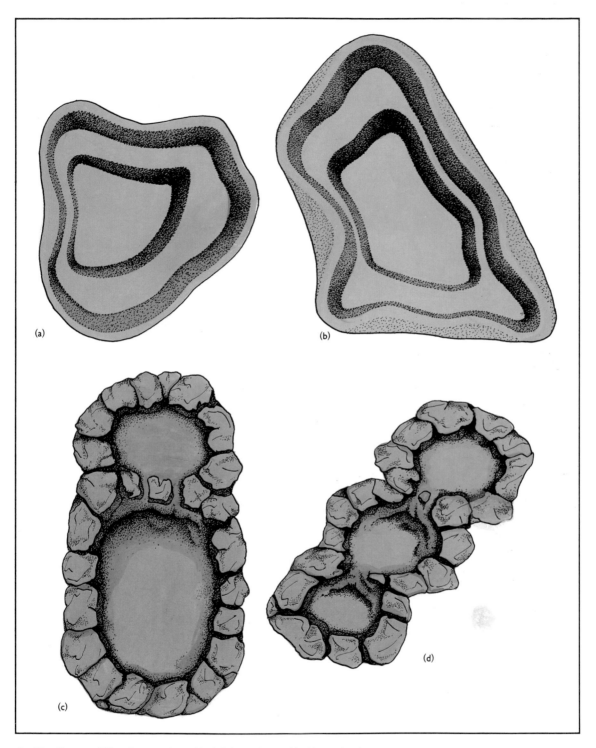

Fig 33   Shapes of fibreglass pond moulds. (a) A simple mould with two levels;
(b) a two-level mould with a framework surround which can be covered with
soil; (c) a mould surrounded by imitation rocks; (d) a fibreglass mould on three
levels to produce a simple watercourse.

liners, and you must be careful when placing them in position not to damage them. Many fibreglass liners are too shallow, so ensure that the one you buy has a large enough area and a depth of 2ft (60cm), to enable you to keep fish and to allow you some choice with your water-lilies.

With fibreglass pools most of the work has been done, and all that you need to do is to excavate a hole 2in (5cm) deeper than the mould and 4in (10cm) wider and longer. (Should you find that you have not got a firm foundation or that there are flints in the soil, excavate to a further depth of 4in (10cm) and replace the earth with damp sand.) Add 2in (5cm) of damp sand to the base (an extra 2in if you have already added 4in), and ensure that the base is absolutely flat with the aid of a spirit level. Drop the mould into place, and put sand

under any gaps formed as a result of the mould design, so that it is on a firm foundation at all points. Place a plank across the top and check with the spirit level that the mould is level. Force sand down the sides of the mould, and then fill with water, checking occasionally with the spirit level to ensure that the mould has not moved. When the pond is filled with water, you should then cover the lips with turves or stones.

Fibreglass moulds are often carelessly sited, with the result that the plastic material protrudes on to the landscape. Unless the container is invisible it will spoil the view, but this is avoidable. Some plastic liners are sold with an edge that is moulded to appear like rocks. When buying such products, you should seek out the very best, otherwise the effect will not be attractive.

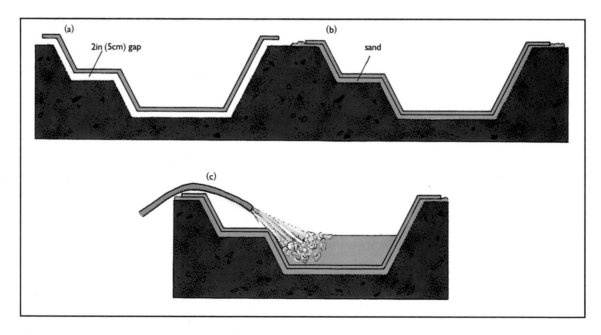

Fig 34   Making a pond with a fibreglass liner. (a) Dig a hole the same shape as the liner, 2in (5cm) larger all the way round. Place a layer of damp sand at the bottom of the hole to act as a smooth level base; (b) push damp sand between the shell and the hole, leaving no air spaces. Check with a spirit level, to avoid the water appearing to settle at an angle, and to prevent stress on the mould; (c) fill slowly with a hose, checking from time to time that the pond remains level. Such a pond should give you years of reliable service.

Fig 35   A raised pond as part of a patio layout.

RAISED PONDS

In spite of the problems associated with very cold spells, raised ponds fit ideally into a terrace landscaping scheme, especially one involving retaining walls and hanging gardens growing in the spaces between the bricks. They are also ideal for the handicapped for whom bending down may present a problem. With a raised pond there is the opportunity to feed and study the fish at your leisure and enjoy the pleasures of gardening without being restricted by disabilities. Raised ponds can be expensive to build. Water exerts a pressure in all directions, so a fairly strong wall is needed to retain this. To contribute to the strength of the structure it will be best to build a concrete pond. The problem here is to produce a structure with a sufficiently high tensile strength, and to guarantee success professional help should be sought.

A plastic or even a fibreglass liner may be used, providing there is a strong retaining wall, built with a 15-degree batter.

An alternative approach to a step-wise garden is to excavate out the soil 2ft (60cm) below the level of the terrain, and build the retaining wall for the whole of the terrace from this depth. Part or all of the lower level of the terrace will now be a water garden. Such an approach provides one of the most efficient uses of a sloping site.

THE SINK POND

Sink gardens, in which an old sink or receptacle of similar size is planted with alpines, cacti or other suitable subjects, and used as an adjunct to the main garden, are a well-established principle. Less familiar are sink ponds. These are miniature pools which are placed in a garden at a suitable position, and fulfil part of the role of the pond, but are insignificant in landscaping terms. No garden is so small that it cannot accommodate a sink pond. In the minutest townscape, the smallest fibreglass liner may be purchased and employed in a miniature layout in a similar fashion to a true pond in a larger area. However, there is one important difference between this and a true water garden — because of the reduced depth and mass of water, freezing solid is a very real possibility and

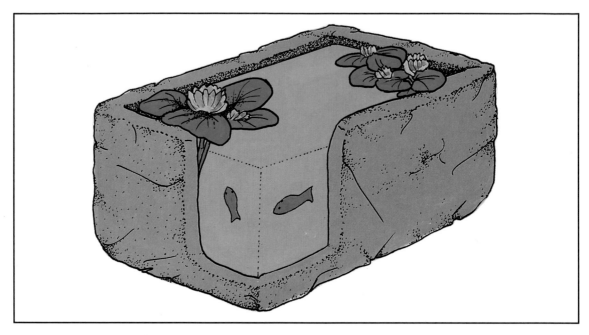

Fig 36   A sink or wooden tub sunk into the ground allows you to enjoy fish
and miniature water-lilies or a wild life haven in even the smallest of plots.

any fish will need to be wintered in an aquarium. This should not cause any disturbance to their development as they can be transferred to an aquarium of a similar size.

To construct a sink pond, simply acquire an old sink – depth is more important than surface area, and you should look out for a vessel at least 9in (22.5cm) deep. Block the drainage hole. If you intend to site the vessel above ground level, remove the glaze from the sink and create a natural-looking finish by roughly covering with a mixture of two parts cement, one part peat, and four parts sand. This will soon age and give an appearance similar to that of natural rock.

You are not restricted here just to sinks, and use can be made of any suitable vessel. Care should be taken to ensure that the vessel is of suitable strength; many plastics will, if exposed to the weather, begin a gradual disintegration, accelerated by the frost. These may not remain outside in the winter, and it will be necessary to store them in a frost-free place in order to protect the material from which they are made. Special containers may be purchased which can be sited outside during the summer months and inside during the winter.

With the sink or miniature pond you will not be able to achieve as much as with a complete pond, but one ideal use is for raising the dwarf water-lily. The vessel functions as a flower pot, with water replacing and taking on the role of the majority of the soil. This is particularly applicable to the patio layout, where special importance is attached to container gardening.

If it is situated in a part of the garden where there is little disturbance, even such a small expanse of water will feature as a natural habitat, and many creatures may be attracted to it. Frogs and newts are no strangers to such sites, and will amply repay you by consuming pests. When you are setting up a miniature natural pond, ensure that you provide an adequate supply of oxygen through water weed.

CHAPTER 3

Establishing the Pond

THE BALANCE OF NATURE

However much we may seek to control it, by providing lilies, other plants and fish that are the result of our manipulative breeding methods, the pond is and will always remain a natural world. It will obey the laws of nature and will be under the control of natural forces. If there is not enough food in the water, fish will die; conversely if there are too many nutrients such as minerals in the water, organisms will colonise it, exploit the food supply, and produce green filamentous algae. Alternatively, micro-organisms may prosper, resulting in a thick, cloudy, soup-like water. If the pond keeper is to be successful he must be aware of this dependence upon nature. It is possible to create the right conditions to direct the natural forces, and this will enable you to produce the effects which you are seeking to achieve.

Fig 37   An attractive well-balanced pond.

Fig 38 *A flourishing well-oxygenated larger pond with a statuette to add a classical touch.*

Oxygen

All living organisms require oxygen to break down the food supply and release energy. There is a far greater oxygen to nitrogen ratio dissolved in water than in the air, because oxygen is more soluble than nitrogen and also because it is liberated by the water weed. Oxygen only dissolves very slowly, and the amount that enters the pond will depend upon the surface area; it is the greatly increased surface area that will lead to absorption of larger quantities of air by water which has been part of a waterfall system or a fountain. As with nutrients, if there is insufficient oxygen the fish

will die, and if there is too much nature will provide other organisms to colonise the area to make use of the excess – these will cloud the water. A gas balance exists and this, as much as the available food, will determine the amount of animal life that the system can support. The amount of oxygen required will depend upon the active mass of life – for example, the amount a fish needs is directly proportional to its size. Species that are very active will need more than those with a calmer life-style, and fish will require far less oxygen in winter, when their metabolic rate has dropped, than in the summer. The greatest demand will be in the breeding season – reproduction is a high-energy activity!

As well as the fish, there are humbler forms of life that make demands on the dissolved oxygen, most importantly decaying material. Decay is brought about by microbes, and these in turn require oxygen for their life processes. The more dead organic material there is in the water, the more of the precious life-giving gas will be consumed. A dead bird or fish could be sufficient to stop the pond from supporting fish, as could the accumulation of leaves and other garden detritus over the autumn and winter months.

Even clear, life-supporting water will not re-main in this state unless steps are taken to ensure that the supply of oxygenated water is constantly regenerated. This can be achieved by the provision of water weeds. These, like all green plants, produce oxygen by photosynthesis, but only during the daylight hours. During the night time they require oxygen themselves to release the stored energy in their cells, so the following morning the oxygen supply will be at its lowest. As the temperature rises, gases (unlike solids) become less soluble in water, and during the summer months, if the pond is stocked to maximum capacity with fish, the oxygen level will be dangerously low and the water should be mechanically aerated. Any method which brings the water into contact with the air – a waterfall, a fountain, or even a pump which pushes air into the water – may be used. As this approach requires regular attention, it is far better to ensure that you do not over-stock with fish. If you wish to maximise the number of fish that you can keep, one way is to have a mechanical aid such as a pump operating permanently.

The level of oxygen will decrease with the depth, and in the lower reaches of a pond life has evolved which does not require free oxygen, but which can make use of the oxygen contained within the energy-giving materials themselves. This way of life 'without air' is termed 'anaerobic respiration'. The microbes which cause decay at the bottom of the pool will live anaerobically, and for this reason the loam or well-rotted manure in which water-lilies are planted will not lead to a reduction in the oxygen level. However, the amount present of such humus material must be carefully controlled, as it will release minerals into the water and these will encourage the growth of water-fouling microbes.

Nutrients

The correct balance of nutrients in the water is the most difficult aspect to achieve. If there are

Fig 39   A pool with the correct balance of nutrients.

too few, you will never produce the lush vegetation and flowers that you require; if there are too many you will encourage so much pond growth that the water will never clear. The single most important factor in attaining and retaining clear water is the correct level of minerals. The roots of bottom-growing plants such as lilies do not take up nutrients, unlike their terrestrial counterparts – their role is purely one of anchorage. The nutrients are taken in by the modified stems, which have an enlarged surface area. Contrasting with this are the floating plants, whose roots have no anchorage function but simply gulp in the minerals that are dissolved in the water. As with all aspects of gardening, some continual form of provision of minerals is essential if any degree of success is to be had. The best method consists of providing a small quantity of well-rotted horse or (preferably) cow manure every three to four years, in the same frequency that is recommended for distribution on the land. This period corresponds with the average length of time that is required to thin out water-lilies. Without realising it, for years gardeners have raised their lilies, replanted in well-rotted manure every three or four years. Only now is science beginning to provide a theoretical understanding to what has been learned over the years by trial, error and observation. The combined effects of the thinning, the encouragement of new growth (which always stimulates any plant), and the addition of nutrients have resulted in water-lilies and other plants of the highest quality. It is a method which is hard to better, if you have some really well-rotted manure, however, this is one instance in which compost is not really a satisfactory substitute.

THE WATER

Tap water contains a quantity of chlorine as well as various dissolved mineral salts, particularly calcium and magnesium. However, the initial filling of your pond may be with tap water, as the water weed will produce oxygen which will quickly replace the chlorine. If the system is allowed a week to a fortnight to settle down, there is very little danger of the gas being present in any significant amount. The mineral salts may be ignored. Once the pond has been filled, the water is under threat from two natural forces: First, evaporation will reduce the volume to an appreciable extent during the summer months, and then there is the problem of rising toxicity. No matter how careful you are, you will not succeed in stopping all of the detritus of the garden from entering the pond. This, together with any waste products that the wildlife builds up, will result in the water becoming progressively less and less suitable for supporting the types of life that we require.

The most effective method of maintaining the sweetness of the water is to have a hose pipe feeding into the pond from the gutters of the house. This will supply water to the pond whenever there is any rainfall, maintaining the level during the summer months without contributing any potentially harmful gases to the system or building up the dissolved solids in the water. Any excess water will run off into the surrounding garden area, and this is ideal if you have included a bog garden in your design. During the winter months the water will enter the pond and an exchange will take place, resulting in a continual replacement of water in the critical top third of the pond. Where it is not considered practical to lead the water straight from the roof to the pond, the rainfall should be collected from the gutter and into a water butt. The pond level can be periodically topped up with this water during the summer. The butt should be allowed to discharge until it is empty during late October and early April, thus ensuring an intermittent replacement of the water.

The amount of water that you will require will depend upon the size of the pond; if it is only small, you will not need the drainage from the whole of the roof. To avoid a greater discharge than the water garden needs, water falling on small areas, such as a shed or a greenhouse, both of which can be fitted with gutters, should be considered. If tap water is the only practical possibility, top up during the summer and treat during autumn and spring as described for rainwater. Check first with the water authority if you do not have a licence for a hose pipe. With a relatively large bog garden a supplementary water supply from the tap will be essential during the summer months, and if you are using tap water there is no reason why you should not route this through the pond itself.

Stagnant Water

Any pond will be incapable of supporting life if the water becomes stagnant. Stagnant water results from large quantities of vegetable matter entering the pond. As well as the system becoming deficient in oxygen, the water will gradually dissolve out increasing amounts of the acid tannin, rendering the medium unsuitable for any forms of life. The usual sign is when the water acquires a brown coloration from the leaves. Natural ponds which are particularly liable to becoming stagnant may additionally acquire a brown coloration if there is any ironstone in the district, as the acid water begins to dissolve the iron out. A third source of brown coloration is certain micro-organisms which contain a pigment of that colour. Another feature which accompanies stagnation is a rainbow effect seen on the top of pond water, due to a very thin film of oil on the surface. The problems of stagnation will be avoided if the water maintenance programme outlined above is followed.

A new pond inevitably takes some time to reach its equilibrium. Once the pond has been filled with water, you should immediately plant the water weeds and water-lilies. At this stage there will be an excess of nutrients and oxygen, and this will inevitably lead to the growth of

Fig 40 *The goodness of this water is illustrated by the healthy fish and plants.*

microbes which will cloud the water. Allow the system about a week to settle down before adding the fish and the water snails. The excess of micro-organisms will be consumed by pond inhabitants, which are soon transported to any new source of water, and in a very short time the water will gradually turn crystal clear. The length of time taken for this will depend upon how quickly the balance of nature can be reached. All changes, such as the replacement of the soil around the lilies or a massive exchange of water in the spring or autumn (where a continual method of replenishing the supply is not used) can lead to a clouding of the water, but the equilibrium will soon be re-established and the water will become clear again. This clouding should never be used as an excuse for not adopting the routine methods of pond maintenance which are essential if the best results are to be achieved.

CHAPTER 4

Plants for Ponds

WATER-LILIES

Water-lilies are by far the most important of the water garden plants, and it is virtually impossible to conceive a pond layout which does not contain at least one type. There are forty to fifty natural species of water-lily throughout the world, and some are tropical, requiring temperatures above those encountered in the average water garden. These need ponds which are artificially heated, or they may be grown in a conservatory or even the house as an aquarium subject. Other species, however, are hardy and can withstand the British climate – one species is even native to Britain. Water-lilies may be found in all of the primary colours, including light blue, and the anthers are often a different colour from the petals, which may vary quite considerably in number. All water-lilies contain four sepals. Some are richly per-

Fig 41   *The water-lily is probably the most popular of all aquatic subjects.*

a disadvantage, as it does allow you to grow some of the more vigorous species in smaller ponds. One simple method of planting is to place the water-lily root, together with a small amount of compost, in a stocking and place this in the pond. Even the small amounts of nutrient from this can lead to an excess of minerals, leading in turn to the growth of large amounts of algae, but the rapid growth of the lilies will soon take over and provide the necessary surface cover to produce clear water.

Water-lilies grow quickly, and they will cover the surface of a pond in three to five years, when they must be thinned out. In May, before there is much growth, remove the old root, and with a sharp knife cut it until you have pieces with three strong eyes (weaker eyes may be removed). Replant in fresh compost. Do not replant unless there has been over-crowding – size rather than time must be the deciding factor, as some species can prosper for many seasons without totally dominating. The exact frequency of replanting varies with the different types.

Varieties to Choose From

Unlike most other garden subjects, you will find that you have room for very few water-lilies – you will probably only be able to have one or two in the size of pond that is most suited to the smaller urban and estate gardens. It is essential that you make the correct choice in the first place, to avoid the expensive need to replace the flowers if you are not content with the variety. You must carefully consider the choice of colours (and there is a large range), because water-lilies are often in very bright shades and must therefore be thought of in terms of their total contribution to the garden. They also vary quite considerably in terms of their coverage and the depth of water that they require. Flower forms differ very much from the open, almost flat, star-shaped varieties, where the sharp petals radiate from the centre to the points of the compass, through the dahlia

Fig 42   Underwater baskets can be useful for planting water-lilies.

fumed. The flowers seem to appear as if by magic from the water, and are brilliantly colour-ed, so it is not surprising that water-lilies feature in the folklore of many peoples.

Growing Water-lilies

Water-lilies require a rich compost, of five parts of good quality loam and one part of well-rotted manure. The mixture may either be deposited at the bottom of the pond and the lilies allowed to root freely, or it may be placed in a container which is little more than a lattice effect allowing the water to circulate. Restricting the roots in a container reduces the vigour of the growth, resulting in smaller plants and reduced pond cover. This is not necessarily

Fig 43   Hardy water-lilies (Nymphaea in variety).

types (there is even a 'water-lily' classification for certain exhibition dahlias), to the tight global-shaped doubles such as 'James Brydon', which imitate the peony. The leaves which appear fresh each spring also vary from pale green through to dark green shot with red. Some varieties have buds of one colour, which open and then gradually change colour. Even the opening of the blooms creates variety, with the water-lily's tendency to open and close with the sun – some types are only open when the sun is at its very brightest, just before and after noon.

Water-lilies are classified by being divided into two groups – the species (those forms which occur naturally in the wild), and the hybrids (the results of crossing species or other hybrids together). Depending upon the variety, water-lilies require different growing depths and, whilst there is often a wide range of water levels which they can tolerate, you should not attempt to grow them in the wrong depth of water. For this reason, where you wish to grow a particular variety you must consider this before designing your pond to ensure that you have suitable conditions. The varying depth can be incorporated to include more than one variety, so that the water-lily is effectively the marginal. Pots may be placed on supports within the pond to artificially create shallower water conditions, if these are required. Because of the importance of the water-lily, especially in formal layouts, the pond should be thought of as the housing for the lily, rather than the lily as a plant to place in the pond.

Fig 44   (Opposite) Pure white is as useful a colour in water gardens as in its terrestrial equivalent.

50

The Species Water-lilies

All water-lily species take the family name *Nymphaea* ('water nymph') and then a second name which usually describes some particular characteristic of the individual species. Sometimes species produce sports or varieties distinct from the usual form, and these are given a third name denoting that variety.

Both species and hybrids can be further sub-divided into hardy and tender. The tender species require varying degrees of artificial heat and are only suitable for ponds which will have a heating system or growing in a conservatory or even as an aquarium 'pot plant', so they need not be considered further. Hybridising records are not complete, so it is not always possible to state with any degree of certainty whether a particular form is a naturally-occurring species or a man-made variety. Some species occurring in the wild may be the result of natural hybridisation.

N. alba   This is the white water-lily, and the only species native to Britain. It is capable of prospering at a depth of 2 – 4ft (60 – 120cm).

N. odorata   The fragrant water-lily, and one of the most important of all varieties in the hybridisation programme. The original white form comes from the U.S.A. Popular varieties include *N. odorata* 'Sulphurea' (a bright, pale yellow variety), and a larger form, *N. odorata* 'Sulphurea Grandiflora' which is extremely fragrant – with flowers of 6in (15cm) or more in diameter, it can appear too large for the smaller ponds. Generally, water-lilies are not strongly fragrant, but either of these will help to attract a large range of insects to the pond.

N. candida   This is a natural white, which is smaller than *N. alba.*

N. fennica   This is a small white form which may have been involved in the production of some of the miniatures.

N. pygmaea alba   The white miniature water-lily. It is probably not a pure species, and may contain either *N. candida* or *N. tetragona* (or both) in its make-up.

N. pygmaea alba 'Helvola'   This is the smallest of all water-lilies, and is a subject especially suited to miniature pond layouts, since it requires a water depth of only 12in (30cm). The flowers are a pale yellow or cream shade.

N. tetragona   A natural miniature with small white flowers.

N. tuberosa   A large water-lily of American origin, which requires quite a deep pond.

The Hybrid Water-lilies

Often the exact origin of a lily is not known; like roses, they may just bear a single name, such as 'Escarboucle' or 'James Brydon', and this will be prefaced by the family name to give 'Nymphaea Escarboucle'. Where the name of the original hybridist is known this is usually commemorated, to give, for example, *Nymphaea x laydekeri* or *Nymphaea x marliacea* (referring to the two Frenchmen, M Laydeker and M Latour-Marliac, pioneers in water-lily cultivar production). This is followed by the name of the variety. As with all plants, the selective hybrids have larger flowers, better form and perfume, brighter colours, and perhaps a longer flowering season than the hybrids. Virtually everyone will find that the hybrids offer better choice and, with the exception of some of the varieties, it is highly unlikely that anyone other than the hybridist will wish to cultivate the species types.

The table opposite shows some of the most popular of the many hardy hybrids available.

BOG PLANTS

Included amongst the recommended species and varieties which may be grown as a part of a water garden are several which may be cultivated away from the water, providing that the soil is kept moist, especially throughout the summer months. Some will even grow in normal herbaceous beds, but they will not prosper unless the moisture level is maintained.

VARIETY	COLOUR	DEPTH OF WATER (in/cm)	REMARKS
'Albida'	White	18–36/45–90	Latour-Marliac hybrid
'Carnea'	Pink to white	18–36/45–90	Latour-Marliac hybrid
'Chromatella'	Yellow	18–48/45–120	Strong-growing, long-flowering Latour-Marliac hybrid
'Escarboucle'	Red	18–24/45–60	One of the most popular of all reds
'Firecrest'	Pale to deep pink	18–24/45–60	Medium-sized flowers
'Frobebelii'	Red	12–24/30–60	A very prolific plant
'Fulgens'	Pinkish red	12–24/30–60	Laydeker hybrid
'Gladstoniana'	White	60–72/150–180	The largest of all the water-lilies
'Helvola'	White	9–12/20–30	The smallest of the water-lilies
'James Brydon'	Pink to rose	12–30/30–75	A very popular hybrid
'Paul Hariot'	Red to pink	12–18/30–45	Vigorous hybrid
'Purpurata'	Pink to red	12–24/30–60	Laydeker hybrid
'Rosea'	Pink to white	18–24/45–60	Latour-Marliac hybrid
'Sunrise'	Yellow to golden	12–18/30–45	Large-flowered cultivar

Fig 45   Flea bane (Pulicaria dysenterica).

Aconitum, Monkshood or Wolf's Bane

This great favourite of the cottage gardener was originally used by the ancient Britons, who dipped their spears into an extract of the roots to kill even the largest wolves – hence the popular name.

However, great care must be taken with this plant, as all parts of it are extremely poisonous, especially the bright red berries which appear after the flowers. *A. napellus*, the European aconitum, has a deep blue hood, and there are many other varieties of the species in cultivation. Plants are transplanted in autumn or the early spring, and flower during July and August, with the berries forming on them about a month later.

Astilbe (Spiraea)

These beautiful plants have feathery pink, white or red flowers made up of a collection of individual florets. The most commonly grown forms are the arendsii hybrids such as 'Bressingham Beauty'. If they are planted during the early spring they will flower from June to September.

Euphorbia palustris

Like all of the euphorbias, this has an almost succulent growth. It flowers from May to June.

Gunnera manicata

No book on water gardening would be complete without an account of this remarkable giant of the wetlands, although very few gardeners will have the room necessary to grow it. *G. manicata* comes from Brazil, but is perfectly hardy in most parts of Britain even in the severest winters. The dead growth of the previous season, after it has died down, is used to cover the roots. The gunnera has one of the largest florescence of any plant and the plant itself, which looks rather like giant rhubarb, will grow to 10ft (3m) in a season. Unfortunately it

will also cover approximately the same area. The yellow flowers form in the early spring, but are not fully developed until the summer. This is very much a subject for the larger garden.

Hosta

A family of Far Eastern plants which are grown almost exclusively for their variegated leaves. The spikes of the flowers are usually in pastel shades, and tend to be insignificant by comparison. Interest in this group of plants is growing rapidly, as they can be grown in herbaceous beds and are an important contribution to colour-co-ordinated displays. There is no shortage of varieties on the market. Under ideal conditions they may grow up to 2–3ft (60–100cm) in height, forming clumps of similar size. Some of the most successful species for grow-

Fig 46   Hostas with their variegated leaves are an important component in the bog garden from May to October.

Fig 47   Mimulus, or the monkey flower, can add colour to your display. It is
eminently suitable for poolside planting.

ing near to water gardens are *H. undulata, H. fortunei* and *H. ventricosa*, but other species should not be ignored. Hostas are cut down by the frosts of autumn and the rootstock, which is perfectly hardy, should be propagated by division before it starts into growth during May.

Lobelia cardinalis

A useful late-season plant. Its bright foliage tinted red, together with the red flowers that appear in September, sustains interest in the water garden until late in the year.

Lysichiton syn. lysichitum

This is another of the arum-like plants which grow so successfully in rich moist ground. The species most frequently in cultivation is *L. americanum* (skunk cabbage), a giant member of the *araceae* family which may attain heights over 4ft (120cm). To achieve such a mass of growth it is necessary to provide large quantities of well-rotted cow or other manure during the spring.

Mimulus sp (*The Monkey flower*)

One of the few genuses that is at home in both alpine and wetland conditions. Flowers are red and yellow, simple or variegated, single or double, depending on which of the several species and their varieties you choose. One of the important advantages of this plant is its ability to flower in August and September. Bog gardens tend to be spring-flowering, and it is therefore important to include these species which extend the season.

55

Fig 48 *Primula denticulata is tolerant of a wide range of conditions and therefore is an ideal waterside plant. It is a firm favourite with all types of water gardens.*

Primulas

The primula family is extremely large and ranges from the alpines, which require a dry open soil, through to the bog or waterside species, which need soil that is rich in humus and never dries out. It is difficult to make generalisations in such a large group, but there is a range of colours in the red to yellow region, as well as some blues. The group tends to flower in the late spring and early summer. The species includes *P. denticulata* with its growth reminiscent of an auricula, which is something of a rarity in that it will prosper in the extremes of the alpine and water gardens. Several varieties of this species (which flowers mainly in

April) do exist. *P. florindae*, an open-type primula rather like a large cowslip, prospers in the water garden and will grow to a height of 3ft (1m). Another very vigorous species is the Japanese primula, *P. japonica*, which can reach heights of 2ft (60cm). For later flowering, plant *P. pulverlum*.

There are several other species of primula that flower in damp conditions, but it is not easy to categorise them simply as either wet or dry land plants. The British native primrose, *P. vulgaris*, prefers damp conditions and is a subject that may be grown safely near to water. There are now several different varieties of *P. vulgaris* some of which are doubles. Many are comparatively recent introductions, and it is not known how successfully all of them fare in very damp conditions. Being waterside subjects, primulas require a soil that is rich in humus. Propagate either by means of plantlets raised in the spring or by root divisions during October. It is more important to have a strong growing rootstock and to allow the minimum amount of disturbance.

Rheum palmatum

A member of the rhubarb family with large feathery leaves. It is only suitable for very large sites as it will grow to 6–9ft (2–3m), with a similar spread.

Trollius

These are members of the *Ranunculaceae* family (as are buttercups). Some of the trollius hybrids display the characteristic globe-shaped flower, whilst others, such as *T. pumulus*, have a flatter, more open flower. The plants may be placed in moist ground during the autumn or winter period, for producing flowers in the following May and June. Deadheading can result in prolonging the flowering period with some types. Seeds of this plant, which should be sown during the early spring, are slow in germinating.

Fig 49 Primula pulverulenta *in a bog garden.*

Fig 50 *The Trollius or globe flower provides yellow buttercup-like flowers in the bog garden throughout May and June.*

DRY BORDERS

A bog garden is by no means essential to the success of the pond, although it is an an extremely useful option, in that it offers the opportunity to grow some very interesting plants which might otherwise be overlooked in garden planning. However, there are other ways of dealing with the land around the pool. One of the most popular of the dry borders is a variation on the alpine theme. With geometrically shaped pools, bright bedding plants may be used as a contrast to the subdued shades of water and the building materials. You should avoid any plants which grow over 1ft (30cm), as they will tend to obliterate the low-growing water-lilies.

Spring

Ideal subjects include *Compositae* (daisies), *Iris reticulata, Narcissii* (various), pansies (winter), *Polyanthus*, snowdrops and tulips (kaufmanniana).

Summer

Try antirrhinums, begonias (both tuberous and fibrous-rooted), lobelia, pansies (summer), *Salvia*, stocks, and *Tagetes*.

Even with two plantings there exists a period from October until March when, unless you are careful, there will only be minimal interest in the ponds, and its surrounds and the garden as a

Fig 51   A pool with a rockery or alpine garden.

Fig 52   Pansies are a very versatile flower and can be used in summer and winter.

whole will look very jaded. In creating a garden for all seasons, water and the surrounding stone will blend well with heather and dwarf conifers. Depending upon the variety, heather will flower from September through to May in a range of whites, purples and reds. Dwarf conifers create year-long interest through their cones, which exhibit the most diverse variety of shapes and tones; new growth will range from a buff shade through to deep red. Green to gold foliage will further enlighten a scene, from the green of *Picea* to the blue of *Juniperus*, with all their mutations in whites, yellows and golds.

However, the most interesting feature is that of form. Dwarf conifers grow in a variety of shapes, which may be based on a column, a cone or a horizontal spread, providing weed-choking ground cover. Careful selection of the various shapes will create a backcloth with perfect balance that will set the pool off and retain its shape (aided if necessary by some judicious pruning) throughout the changing of the seasons.

In any garden during the dark days of November through to January, apart from a few straggling species of winter cherry, Chinese

Fig 53 *Tagetes add a colourful splash to a dry border.*

witch hazel and *Viburnum*, there is little to create interest other than the heathers and conifers. These can be used as part of a raised mound in conjunction with a small quantity of stone. The stone is present purely for visual effect, and the structure should not be confused with a rockery where more stone is used with an important ecological contribution to make. Such a feature is not intended to produce colour in the manner of a summer bedding surround, none the less you may need to add to it to maintain interest during bright days of spring and summer. Plant a few very bright subjects, such as snowdrops, miniature narcissi and gentians, being careful not to over-plant.

With a dry border such as this drainage is essential, but it is important to keep everything in proportion – too large a structure will not be in keeping with the smaller pool most suited to the urban garden. Aim to raise the bed no more than 3ft (1m), and at the centre of the mound place brick rubble and other drainage materials before covering with top soil. This should be of good quality loam, and part of the soil excavated for the pond itself may be used. Add a handful of bonemeal per surface square yard of the mound, to provide the slow-release nutrients that are so important with trees and shrubs. Do not add any general fertiliser as this will result in fast, soft growth, which will be incapable of withstanding the winter.

Your dry border can be the ideal setting for a watercourse. Again, this illustrates the importance of considering all the design aspects of water gardening together.

MARGINALS

These are plants which prefer to grow with their roots permanently under between 2 and 6in (5 – 15cm) of water. Despite this fact, they are land plants, and they will have a rapidly spreading rootstock. Left unchecked, the stronger varieties – many of which are British natives perfectly adapted to the conditions – will rapidly take over. You could simply cover the bottom of the pond with rich compost and plant, but the result will be the same as in a garden where a subject such as couch grass has been allowed to grow out of control. It is far better to plant the marginals in containers; not only does this tend to slow down the growth, but it will also provide a finite boundary to the plant's terrestrial ambitions. Care should be taken in the selection of containers and they should be fully compatible with the material from which the pond itself is constructed. With concrete ponds, brick or block troughs can be made at the time of construction, divided into sections of the correct size for each of the intended species. With fibreglass or sheet plastic, bought plastic troughs are best. Troughs should be about 9in (22.5cm) high, and two-thirds filled with a mixture of two parts good friable loam

Fig 54 Marginal planting showing Mimulus cardinalis *and* Primula florindae.

Fig 55 Baskets such as these can be used as plant containers under the surface of the water.

and one part well-rotted manure. Cover with about 2in (5cm) of pea gravel. This serves to stop the fish from disturbing the soil and clouding the water.

Design

A collection of marginals in the water is the equivalent of the herbaceous border on land and the same rules of composition will apply. This is often usually disregarded in the design of water gardens, and the collection appears as a jungle. The layout should be plotted out on paper, with the siting of the troughs, if these are to be permanent features (if not, they may be moved around as plant holders are on a patio). Site the marginals farthest from the viewing eye, so that they do not obstruct the view.

A good basic design for the larger water garden is based upon the kidney shape; not

Fig 56 Juncus effusus *'Spiralis'*, or corkscrew rush,
makes a fine foliage plant at water margins.

only does this form engender interest in itself, but it has a large front area compared with the back, and an open front construction allowing the observer to see into the bed, and it also allows the largest area in which to grow tall subjects without obstructing the view. Allow 3ft (1m) in height for the 'backcloth'. A *Typha*, or reedmace makes an excellent central subject, with irises, *Sagittaria* or *Peltandra* as the supporters. In front of these, three or four of the smaller species – *Calla*, *Caltha*, *mentha aquatica* and *Myosotis* – are all suitable.

There is not a vast range of marginals, and the colours are less bright than with the terrestrial species, so there is far less danger of colour clashes within the bed. With the dark green of the vegetation, and the water in the foreground, and the fact that the plants do not all flower together, this aspect may safely be ignored. This is not to say that the marginals cannot create dramatic effect – the marsh marigold, for example, should always be given sufficient room at the front of the display, as it greets the spring with a dazzling display of golden cups. You will almost certainly be restricted to only one water bed, and this will have to sustain interest throughout the year, so choose from the following plants to provide a succession of flowers from March to September.

***Calla palustris* (bog arum)** This acquires its popular name from the white arum-shaped flowers which are pollinated by water snails. These are followed by red arum-type berries in August. A British native.

***Caltha* sp (marsh marigold, kingcup)** Prefers a slightly acid soil (pH 6.0 – 6.5), rich in humus, such as would be found in its natural

Fig 57   The marsh marigold is a favourite water garden plant.

habitat. *C. palustris* 'Alba' is a white and *C. palustris* 'Plena' is a double yellow.

Iris kaempferi   Arguably the most majestic of all marginals, irises adorn the edge of the pond as water-lilies do the middle. They flourish in 3 – 4in (7 – 10cm) of water. Flowers early summer, and may be obtained in shades of white and yellow. *I. laevigata* is slightly smaller than *I. kaempferi*, but is a true marginal, preferring about 4in (10cm) of water. It is of the deepest shade of blue, and there is a white

variety, 'Alba'. The yellow iris seen in ponds and on river banks in the British countryside is *I. pseudacorus*.

Mentha aquatica (water mint)   This prefers shallow water, and is almost a bog subject. It produces pinkish-blue flowers in late spring and early summer, and has a pleasant aromatic smell. It is very easy to cultivate.

Menyanthus trifoliate (bog bean)   A vigorous marginal preferring 2 – 3in (5 – 7cm) of water. Produces a carpet of pink flowers in

Fig 58 The yellow flag (Iris pseudacorus) flowers throughout June.

Fig 59 Gypsy wort and water mint (Lycopus europaeus and Mentha aquatica).

May and June. This plant has a spreading habit and it must be ruthlessly thinned each year, otherwise it will take over the site completely.
Myosotis palustris syn. M. scorpioides (water forget-me-not) This has a leaf and flower similar in shape to the terrestrial forget-me-not, but flowers in July long after the latter has ceased, and at a time when there is a declining interest in the water garden. This makes it a must for virtually all informal ponds. It is a British native.
Peltandra sp. Like the bog arum, to which this plant is closely related, Peltandra have arum-like flowers and berries. If this is the effect you are seeking, in the majority of small gardens you would be better advised to grow the smaller Calla palustris.

Ranunculus lingua 'Grandiflora' (spear-wort) It is easy to see how the common name arose as this plant appears very much like a spear growing out of the water. It flowers early to mid-summer, producing golden-yellow buttercup-type flowers up to 2in (5cm) across.
Sagittaria (arrowhead) The leaves have the characteristic shape of an arrowhead. There are several different species but the one which is most commonly in cultivation is S. sagittifolia. It favours fairly deep water – 1 – 3ft (60 – 100cm), the white flowers occurring during mid-summer. Set out the small plantlets or root cuttings during mid-summer, and take care to remove excess roots annually, as this is a plant which can take over a pond. British native.

Fig 61   Frogbit.

Stachys palustris (marsh woundwort)
A perennial plant with many leaves, producing red flowers towards the end of the season.

Typha sp (reed mace)   This plant is often mistaken for the bulrush. It is without peer for floral arranging, and *T. latifolia* can grow in water as shallow as 6in (15cm) or as deep as 3ft (1m). In good rich soil its height can exceed 6ft (2m). It should be planted away from the observer, and in design terms it fulfils the same role as a tree in a garden, giving mass and height to the scene. This is another vigorous grower which, unless kept in check, will take over the whole pond, so it is not a subject for the smaller water garden layout. *T. latifolia* and *T. angustifolia* are both British natives.

Zantedeschia aethiopica   Another of the water plants with an arum lily-type florescence. In the spring it has a white flower with a yellow centre. The variety 'Crowborough' is the one that is most frequently grown.

FLOATING PLANTS

These are plants whose leaves float on the surface of the water, usually with the roots moving freely in the water and absorbing nutrients from it. They have no anchorage.

Aponogeton distachyos (water hawthorn)
The popular name is derived from the perfume that the plant emits. It has egg-shaped leaves which float on the water, and flowers throughout the summer months.

Eichhornia crassipes (water hyacinth)
This is one of the most beautiful of water plants, its popular name deriving from the pale blue hyacinth-like spikes of flowers. Unfortunately it is a tender subject and must be kept inside under frost-free conditions during the winter.

Hydrocharis   morsus-ranae   (frogbit)
Small white flowers.

Nuphar   Yellow flowers not unlike a celandine, with both floating and submerged leaves. Flowers throughout the summer.

Nymphoides (floating heart)   Not to be confused with the water-lilies *Nymphaea*. Yellow flowers from summer through till the autumn. Tolerant of a wide range of water depths.

Trapa natans (water chestnut)   This is a tender annual plant which is grown for its attractive leaves. It is propagated by seeds.

Fig 60   *The water hawthorn with its delicate pink and white flowers appearing above the surface of the water in the early spring has a magical, almost mystical aura.*

CHAPTER 5

Pond Life

KEEPING FISH

The vast majority of pond owners will want to keep fish. These vibrant and often spectacular forms of life, one minute basking in the sun and the next darting about the pond like metal flashes, really are pets. Once they have confidence in their owners they will take food from the hand, and come at a certain time of day to the part of the pond where they are accustomed to being fed. Fish always attract atten-

tion in any garden, whether it is a large landscape area or a small surburban patch. The Chinese, great pond builders, started the process of selective breeding to obtain the most spectacular forms of fish. This process has been greatly advanced in the twentieth century since the theory of genetics has been understood, and now we have forms of goldfish that are far removed from their wild ancestors. Often, however, the most exciting types – the brightest-coloured, or those with the most elaborate

Fig 62   A carp can become very tame and eat from the hand.

Fig 63   *Water-lily leaves provide goldfish with camouflage from predators and protection from the sun.*

fin structure – are the most difficult to raise, precisely because they are so far removed from the natural forms. Elaborate fin structures, for example, come at the expense of the speed necessary to catch prey in competition with other, more streamlined types. Similarly, they may lack the speed needed to escape a predator (the bright colours usually favoured by pond keepers offer no camouflage), or they may be incapable of withstanding the severest winter.

Even the most difficult of fish can be raised if you make the effort and take the necessary steps to provide for their special requirements. Cover and a certain amount of protection can be provided in the form of a bridge, or a drainpipe, or simply by carefully breaking a flower pot laterally in two.

Winter

The majority of fish that are kept in ponds are members of the carp family. The breeding of ornamental carp originates from China, but the farming of carp in Britain dates back to at least the Middle Ages when they were raised in monasteries for food. Their rearing and keeping usually presents no problem as most are able to withstand our harshest winters – some, noticeably the fantail, will require extra heat. During the winter months organic materials in the pond will continue to decompose as a result of bacterial action on the floor of the pond, resulting in a build-up of the gases methane, ammonia and the lethal hydrogen sulphide. At the same time, the fish will be using up the oxygen which is stored in the water. It is important, therefore, that even during the

67

Fig 64   A wide variety of fish including Koi carp.

severest spells of cold weather an exchange of the gases can take place and a space is kept open. The most practical way of achieving this is to place an old tennis ball on the surface of the pond. The small currents and the wind will cause the ball to move about, and this movement will stop the water in that small area freezing.

This alone will be effective in milder areas, and in all but the severest of winters, but there will be occasions when the water freezes even around the ball. An ice-hole must be opened immediately, by clearing any snow away and pouring boiling water into a large tin can resting on the surface to melt the ice. You must not attempt to crush the ice, as this will create

Fig 65   To make a hole in the ice sufficiently
large for the exchange of gases to take place,
place a can on the surface and pour near-boiling
water into it. The rubber ball relieves some of the
pressure created by the ice.

compression waves in the water which may kill the fish.

A far more reliable method of saving your fish in the winter is to purchase a small electrical pond heater which can be connected to the mains. These are extremely economical to run, and are only switched on during a cold spell or when one is expected. They are not of course designed to raise the temperature of the whole pond, but only of a small area. The slight localised rise in temperature will ensure that a small hole remains open through the ice during even the coldest spells. This will be sufficient for the necessary exchange of gases to occur.

Stocking with Fish

The number of fish that you can keep will depend upon the quantity of oxygen dissolved in the water, which will in turn depend upon the surface area and the amount of water weed. Whilst the amount of water weed will to some extent depend upon the depth, it is not the case that double the volume of pond water means that you can keep twice as many fish. A far better method to determine the number of fish which can be kept is based on the surface area of the pond. A large fish of about 6in (15cm) will use up approximately twice the oxygen of one half its size, but that small fish will, given time, grow to the full size for its species. To avoid over-crowding at a later stage, you should under-estimate the space available. You can always add extra fish. *Never have more than one fish per 2–3 sq ft (0.3 sq m).* Koi carp grow much larger than many, and if you wish to raise them to full size you should not stock at a rate greater than *one fish per 20–25 sq ft (2–3 sq m).* They are not a subject for the small garden pond!

Any sudden change in their environment leads to stress in fish, which can kill them or lower their resistence to disease. To avoid a sudden temperature change, allow the fish to remain in the transporting container and water until it reaches ambient temperature. Gently place the container and fish in the pond, tilting so that the fish may swim out.

Fig 66   When stocking with fish carefully maintain a consistent environment.

Fish Breeding

Fish breeding is often thought of as an unplanned accident, however, with a little care and forethought, it is possible to increase your chances of successfully raising the young fish to adulthood. Few people will wish to raise their fish to exhibition standards – if you do then you will need to direct all of the pond's activity toward this aim, and you will require a good working knowledge of genetics. Most people will prefer simply to breed fish and dispose of them to the local pet shop.

The sexing of goldfish is so difficult for the inexperienced as to be virtually impossible. Whilst it is true that the male has tubicles (growths) on its gills, to see these it is necessary to catch the fish and move aside the perinitum, an operation that can damage the fish, and create a point of entry for disease. Immediately prior to breeding the female will become swollen with eggs, and viewed from above she will seem to be much wider than the male. However, the size of goldfish is a very complex matter, depending, amongst other factors, on the nature of the environment. They are even capable of suspended growth – a goldfish can live for many years in an aquarium and never exceed about 5cm (2in), but on release into a pond will rapidly grow. (The reason for this is not fully understood, but the growth may be suspended as a result of the stress of living in an alien environment.) During the breeding season (which is dependent upon both the temperature and number of daylight hours, and runs from late April until August) it is possible to touch the female in the vent region, discharging a small quantity of eggs. The male will then emit a small amount of milk-like sperm.

Goldfish breed in groups and do not readily fight, so do not be worried about an overprovision of either sex. The best way of ensuring that you have both a male and a female is to include three fishes in the pond – the odds against having only one sex are one in four; if you have four fish then the odds are one in

Fig 67 Small goldfish bought from a pet shop will rapidly grow in a pond.

eight. Goldfish are ornamental carp, and the majority of carp will breed with each other. However, where the breeds are the same the chances of them breeding successfully are far greater. The common goldfish sold in pet shops is sufficiently hardy to survive our winters, and these same fish, so often thought of as only suitable for the aquarium, will happily breed in a pond. Ornamental fish are the result of selection and do not always breed true, and less colourful young may occur as recessive genes reappear in future generations. Should you wish to obtain fish that will breed true, ensure that you obtain your stock from a specialist supplier who will advise you on your needs.

Goldfish do have a breeding season. The specimen trapped in a bowl will not notice the passing of the year, but the pond dweller exposed to the elements will experience a slowing-down of his metabolism as the cold weather approaches. During the winter months it will eat very little, living mainly off the fat that it has stored in its body. Where the fish has an abundance of food, such as in the garden pond, this period is essential to bring about a reduction in body weight. It is the rise in temperature immediately after the cold period that stimulates the breeding activity. Ideally the breeding group should be established in position the previous autumn so that there is no sudden change of conditions which could upset the breeding cycle. During the spring or summer, when the female is swollen with spawn, the male will approach her and, by movements of his body near to hers, induce her to deposit the eggs on to nearby water weed, which are then externally fertilised. From the moment the spawn leaves the female's body it is in danger, falling prey to any adult fish and various other predators, so you need to spot the spawn as soon as it is laid (you may safely assume that it has been fertilised) and transfer it to an aquarium where the fry can be raised safely. Goldfish will eat their own eggs virtually as soon as they are laid, and this explains why the fish in some stocked ponds never increase in number. Occasionally one will survive the egg and fry stage, but over-crowding does greatly reduce the chances of the young surviving.

Start looking out for the eggs in late April or May on water weeds or the underside of floating plants. Goldfish do not like spawning in temperatures below 59°F (15°C), but look every day, otherwise the eggs will disappear. If you harvest the eggs at the correct time you will have more than enough for your purposes. In the pond no special food is required for the fish, which will readily feed off the minute organisms present, but in the aquarium special food must be supplied.

Raising the Eggs

Inside every fertile egg there is an embryo which needs oxygen. This passes through the wall of the egg, with the waste gases passing out in the opposite direction. It is therefore important that the water is well oxygenated, and, if you intend raising a large quantity of young, you will need an oxygenator (obtainable from most pet shops) for your aquarium. For small-scale fish rearing experiments (and it is always better to raise a smaller quantity than to risk losing all the young through over-crowding), simply set up the aquarium with gravel and water weed in the usual way. The temperature of the water should be 65–70°F (18.5–21°C). Remember that in a pond fluctuations are only slight, compared with an aquarium, where there is far less volume of water, and a much greater surface area through which the heat can be lost following the slightest change in ambient temperature. The young will hatch after 4–5 days. Any eggs remaining 3 days after the first ones have hatched, or ones which have fallen to the bottom of the aquarium, will almost certainly be infertile and should be removed immediately before they begin to decay and pollute the water.

Raising the Fry

When the young emerge they will have the yolk sac attached and this will be sufficient food for the first few days, but then you should provide the yolk of a boiled hen's egg. It is very important that you do not over-feed. Excess food will break-down and use up some of the available oxygen. After a week of egg yolks, gradually provide other food, but only that which is small and soft. The goldfish should remain in the aquarium system until at least ten weeks old, and as they get older they will require additional quantities of oxygen. With large numbers of goldfish, either set up additional aquaria, or cull so that you are left only with those fish that have the best appearance. Once they have reached adulthood the young may be returned to the pond, but only if there is sufficient room.

Food for Goldfish

Fish will acquire much of the food that they need from natural sources. Minute crustacea, insects and mosquito larvae all contribute to the diet, but you may need to supplement this. Give small amounts of any of the proprietary fish foods. Pelleted foods are compounded to

Fig 68   Care must be taken not to over-feed fish.

provide an exact balance of the nutrients re-quired, but take care not to over-feed. Provide no more food than you can comfortably hold between your thumb and forefinger. Ensure that the fish eat all of it, and clear away any that is not consumed. Surplus food will rapidly begin to decompose and cause a clouding of the water. This decomposition will release nitrogen and other minerals which will encourage the growth of micro-organisms causing further clouding.

Generally, the rate at which a fish grows and uses up food will depend upon the tempera-ture, although above a certain temperature it will begin to slow down again. In addition, the fish will consume more food in the spring when they are producing eggs, but this will be partially compensated for by their tendency to eat their own eggs and by the abundance of wild food present. The summer will generally be a time of high food intake, due to the breeding season extending to August, and the building up of reserves for the winter. Because of the reduced metabolic rate during the winter months, pro-viding the fish are healthy there will be no need to feed them, and they probably will not take food even if it is offered.

Goldfish *(Carassius auratus)*

No fish is better suited to live with man than the goldfish. It can survive the ordeal of being transported from a fun fair in a small plastic bag and, after being unceremoniously deposited in a pond, may live for years. However, this is not a recommended way of obtaining your speci-mens. If they remain in such a bag for any period of time they will die through lack of oxygenated water, and fish from unknown sources always carry the risk of bringing disease with them. There is no substitute for buying your fish from a reputable dealer. As a bonus he will usually be able to provide any extra advice that you might require.

The goldfish is too well known to require any detailed description, with its metallic scales in a wide range of colours. Under ideal condi-tions it will grow to a maximum length of 4–5in (10–12cm). The common goldfish is the variety best suited to most ponds and will live trouble free for many years. Modern breeding has led to distinct varieties of goldfish.

Shubunkins   These have a gene missing, the one that is responsible for the metallic lustre, and they also carry the blue factor. This pro-duces a range of apparently scaleless fish in a wide range of colours. They tend to be no more difficult to raise than the common goldfish and may be recommended to the novice fish keeper.

Comet   This is a variety of the shubunkin, with a rear fin which can be almost half of the total length of the fish, and no anal fin. The more subdued colours, and the greater agility afforded by the modified rear fin, makes this a variety which is particularly well suited to sur-vival; like all shubunkins it is hardy. This is another fish which can be recommended to all pond keepers.

Fantail   This is a form of goldfish which re-tains the metallic sheen, with the distinguishing characteristic of an almost egg-shaped body curving into the downward-facing caudal fin. It

Fig 69   There are many types of goldfish to choose from.

Fig 70   Koi carp are very popular.

is a fish of great beauty, however, it is not sufficiently hardy for Britain unless the pond is heated. It is sometimes suggested that this form can be transferred to an aquarium in winter, but this is not satisfactory as it can lead to different rates of growth, and because the fantail will soon out-grow all but the largest aquaria.

Veiltail   A variety of the fantail with a far more elaborate caudal fin consisting of a series of folds. This slows the fish down considerably and makes it difficult to rear, so it should only be considered by the experienced fish keeper.

Golden orfe   This is one of the most stream-lined of all species. A bright reddish-gold in colour, it is an ideal subject for the larger pond.

Koi carp (*Cyprinus carpio*)   These are great favourites in large gardens that are open to the public, where their colouring, size and darting movements provide constant interest. These Japanese fish can easily be raised at home, providing you have a sufficiently large and deep pond. If the conditions are ideal some may grow to almost 3ft (1m) in length, so they do require a fairly large pond! Because of their specialist requirements they cannot be recommended for an owner of a small garden pond, and even if you were able to provide a suf-

ficiently large area of water, it is unlikely that you could provide a design capable of retaining the balance between a sufficiently large water garden and its surroundings. To prosper carp need room to move, and a depth of 4–5ft (1.5m) of water. Such a depth will prohibit the growth of some water-lilies, but it does open up the possibility of growing the spectacular *N. grandiflora*. The large fish, with their high energy movement, will metabolise large amounts of oxygen, only part of which can be successfully produced by water weeds. Providing you stock at a rate of no more than one fish per 20–25 sq ft (2–3 sq m). there is no need to aerate the water artificially, although it is advisable to provide a fountain. A significant amount of oxygen may also be obtained through a waterfall in the system. A fountain or waterfall should be working in the morning when the oxygen supply has been used up during the night.

Minnows (*Phoxinus phoxinus*)

For anyone who is interested in raising British native fish, the easiest to begin with is the humble minnow, which will only grow to about 3in (7–8cm) in length. The barrel-shaped fish prefers to live in a shoal and its darting movement appears as silver flashes in the water – a random movement that is totally coherent within the group itself. Over the years millions of these tiny fish have perished through lack of oxygen, as a result of being transported and kept in jam jars by eager youngsters. If they are quickly transferred from the wild to the garden pond they will immediately accept their new environment. During the spring the female will lay her eggs. These will hatch in 9–12 days and the shoal size will settle down to the maximum number that the size of the pool and the food supply can accommodate. Being natives they are perfectly hardy, although it will be necessary to remove the ice from the water during cold spells.

SNAILS

Water snails will feed on any excess of food and the general detritus of the pond. These scavengers are essential if you are to have any hope of keeping the water clear.

The ramshorn snail *(Planorbis corneus)* is light brown, flat and coiled. It is totally hardy, available from all aquarium suppliers, and an hermaphrodite which will breed readily in your pond. However, the small white eggs, which soon develop black spots of the growing embryos and which are laid throughout the spring and summer, will often be eaten by fish

and other predators. Ultimately it is the food supply which will determine the number that the pond will support. It will be about a year before a true balance is established, but for a medium-sized pond you should initially buy between three and five snails. Other types of water snail should not be considered as they may graze off cultivated vegetation.

WATER WEEDS

If your pond is to sustain life, it must have water weeds growing in it. These are the plants which oxygenate the water during the daytime. The role of the roots is one of anchorage, with nutrients being absorbed through the stem, and gravel is the ideal rooting medium. Fill a large ceramic flower pot with gravel and place pieces of water weed in the rooting medium. Carefully lower the container-grown plants into position. For water weeds to prosper they must be planted in a position that receives maximum sunlight. The amount of oxygen that the weeds produce will depend upon how much light can penetrate the water.

Callitriche platycarpa (starwort) Can form an underwater jungle which should be cut back to manageable proportions each summer. Due to its vigorous growth, it is a useful plant for the larger pond.

Ceratophyllum demersum An oxygenator which can survive at depth, where less sunlight penetrates. Probably the best plant for shaded parts of the pond.

Elodea canadensis (Canadian pondweed) The most popular of all oxygenating plants. A prolific grower which spreads rapidly and which requires drastic cutting back during August and September.

Lagarosiphon major syn. Elodea crispa Very similar to *E. canadensis* in growth and habit.

Myriophyllum sp. A genus of oxygenating plants which produce small insignificant in-

Fig 71   Common duckweed. In other than a natural pond this is considered to be a weed and must be removed periodically.

Fig 72   Whorled water milfoil.

florescence above water level. *M. spicatum* has minute red flowers, and others lime green flowers. Not one of the better oxygenating families.

Ranunculus aquatilis (common water crow-foot)   As well as the submerged oxygenating parts, the plant also produces floating leaves and small yellow buttercup-shaped flowers during the summer.

IN THE NATURAL WATER GARDEN

Ponds are one of the fastest of all natural features to disappear from the landscape, and natural ponds built into gardens are a recent innovation, the contribution of man to the pre-servation of natural species under threat. The

Fig 73 *Natural water gardens are an important ecological aspect of the environment.*

area covered by gardens in Britain is in excess of a million acres, and, if the wild life of the country is to survive and co-exist with man, it is imperative for urban gardens to be enticing for the creatures of the natural world. No area is too built up to attract wild life, and the importance of man providing help is beyond dispute. It has been estimated that the frog population of the British Isles is only one per cent of what it was before the Second World War, and this illustrates the uphill struggle facing certain species.

However, do not be *over*-enthusiastic in your efforts to attract wild life to your garden; *never* raid a natural habitat for either adult endangered species, such as the amphibians, or their eggs or young, as this is an offence for which there is a very heavy fine.

A natural pond is the same as a basic ornamental fish pond, with the fish omitted. This does not mean that the pond can be neglected, as even indigenous species will not survive where leaves are decaying. Your pond will require ecological management by which you seek to attract species into the garden. You do not have to make special provision, because many creatures will enter your garden of their own volition, but it does help. Plant water weeds to provide the necessary oxygen for the eco-system, and provide other plants, such as natural marginals and bog subjects. Again, do not raid natural habitats, but seek out the specialist suppliers. The pond is a total environment with many long and complex food chains, so stocks of minute organisms – algae, water fleas and freshwater shrimps – will build up first, and then higher animals will gradually be attracted to the area. The process may be

Fig 74   Brooklime (Veronica becabunga).

Fig 75   Detail of the ecological garden on a smaller site.

Fig 76 Insects such as the water soldier (Stratiotes aloides) will soon colonise such an area.

speeded up by taking samples of pond water from natural ponds, and adding these samples to the bulk of the water. Then transfer some natural weed to the pond. The aim is to attract visiting pond-loving species rather than to imprison them; providing the conditions are right, you will ultimately attract at least some of the higher forms of pond life to the water. It is also possible on occasions legally to acquire either eggs or tadpoles when there is a site shortly to be developed or where there is an overstock in a particular area. Contact your local conservation society (find their address in the local library), and they will inform you of any nearby sources.

Once the pond is laid out it will begin to attract migrants — few at first (perhaps honey bees stopping for a drink), then butterflies and, with luck, a dragonfly. Caddis flies, with their several different forms, will all ultimately come to your pond, as will a wide range of birds. You may even attract a kingfisher. Your pond is the start of your own nature reserve.

The Amphibians

All the amphibians tend to spend the breeding season in or near to water. As the summer progresses they spend more and more time on land with a marked preference for damp ground. Young frogs linger near the area where they were tadpoles, but as they get older they will venture forth to colonise new areas. During October they start their annual hibernation under damp stones. Amphibians lay their eggs in water and these hatch into tadpoles (or efts, in the case of newts), which metamorphise into the adult form in a matter of weeks. They are all carnivores, frogs consuming large quantities of slugs and harmful insects, and newts eating mainly insects and worms. Both, therefore, are extremely useful in the totally organic garden where no pesticides are employed.

Common frog (Rana temporana) This is the only frog that is likely to find its way into your garden, and during March it may be heard croaking on the pond. Its breeding season is from March to May, when it lays its eggs in clumps, once the temperature has reached 48°–50°F (9–10°C).
Common toad (Bufo bufo) This is the only other frog-like creature that you are likely to encounter in the garden, and it is readily distinguished from the frog by the large number of warts all over its body. The toad lays its eggs in long strings about a month after the frog has started, and they seem to get caught up in the water weed. Whether the frog or toad will be the more common in your garden depends upon the locality.

Great crested newt (*Triturus cristatus*) The rarer of the two British native newts, this is the larger and the male has a crest running along its back. Its breeding period lasts from March to June. It is by no means unknown in garden ponds, but its appearance should be considered as a bonus rather than something which can be planned.

Smooth newt (*Triturus vulgaris*) As its scientific name implies, this is the common newt (although despite its name is becoming increasingly rare), and the one you are most likely to attract into your garden. It is only two-thirds of the size of the great crested newt. Newts tend to stay near water far longer than frogs and are amongst the most interesting of the natural pond creatures.

Frogs, toads and newts seldom prosper in the same pond, especially a small one, probably because they are all competing for the same food supply. Artificial introduction of any of these species is best achieved at the tadpole stage.

Other Creatures

Great pond snail (*Lymnaea stagnalis*) As well as feeding off dead and decaying material, this snail, which looks like a unicorn's horn, will graze off the vegetation. For this reason, it should never be included in any pond · where there has been a planting of ornamental vegetation, especially water-lilies. However, the ramshorn snail, which feeds entirely on dead material, may be included in either type of pond.

Water stick insect (*Ranatra linearis*) A long, thin insect which preys on other insects and tadpoles. The adults can both swim and fly and will rapidly colonise any pond. It should not be considered a pest, as it helps to maintain the balance of nature and destroy those herbivores which would feed off the vegetation.

Water boatman (*Sigara lateralis*) This is a very common brown-black insect which flies at night. There is also the common *corixa* which is often referred to as a water boatman. The latter is an oval-shaped insect with a steel blue body, which goes to the surface to breathe and seems to be suspended by the surface tension.

Water scorpion (*Nepa cinerea*), **Saucer bug** (*Illyocoris cimicoides*), and **water singer** (*Micronecta poweri*). These may all appear in any pond, although the larger the pool the greater the variety of these and similar species.

Caddis fly (*Trichoptera* sp.) These insects, of which there are several species, are somewhat similar to moths in appearance. Of particular interest is the caterpillar which often has a tubular case to protect it, covered with grains of sand, twigs and various natural debris, effecting a camouflage.

Beetles and spiders There are several species of both of these which live either in or around water. The most fascinating is probably the water spider (*Argyroneta aquatis*), which builds a diving bell of silk which it then fills with air. It lives, mates and lays its eggs within this diving bell. The common pond skater (*Gerris lacustris*) is to be found on virtually every pond. The adult is unable to fly, so it uses the surface tension, and literally walks on water. The little pond skater (*G. argentatus*) and the tolland pond skater (*G. odontogaster*) both have a similar appearance and life-style, and are also very common. The water measurer (*Hydrometra stagnorum*) and lesser water measurer (*H. gracilenta*) are similarly surface dwellers which are widely distributed.

Mussels Freshwater mussels are vegetarians living mainly on algae and will obviously not survive unless there is an adequate supply. For this reason mussels should only be placed in an established pond where they will help in the maintenance of clear water. The mussel most frequently added to the garden pond is the highly attractive 'painter's mussel'. These can be purchased from a limited number of specialist suppliers.

CHAPTER 6

Other Features

MOVEMENT

The water garden should be seen in terms of the landscape as a whole and the contribution which it makes to the total vista, and water is indispensable in a landscape because it is capable of providing both movement and sound. In large gardens professional designers exploit the beauty of moving water to the full, providing dazzling displays of fountains and waterfalls. A similar effect is possible in the small garden providing attention is paid to the scale and balance of the plot. It is not impossible to design a garden without the element of water, but it is unlikely that the fullest potential of the site will be realised if it is omitted.

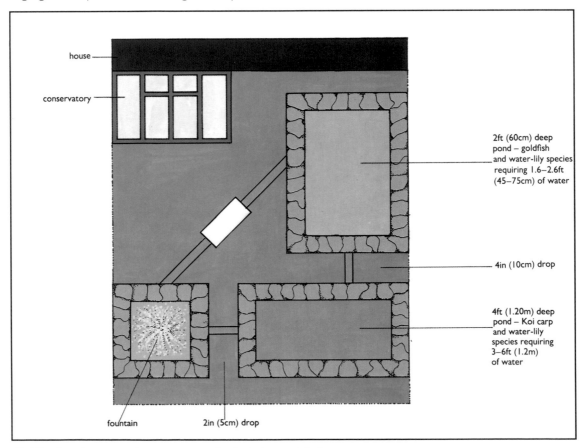

Fig 77   A total water garden concept providing both deep and shallow water.

Fig 78   A water garden with plenty of movement, surrounded by rockery plants such as Armeria, Mimula *(which also thrives in bog conditions), and* Campanula.

Natural rises and slopes that the designer chooses not to level are obvious sites for a waterfall, and where such natural contours do not exist they can be created artificially, from the material excavated in the building of the pond (see page 32). One approach is to attempt to create a watercourse reminiscent of an alpine scene with the whole of the area almost covered in granite or limestone. Less ambitious but equally effective visually is to rely on splash trays to drop the water to a lower level. All watercourses depend upon the ability to lift water, and the most fundamental of all questions that any gardener must ask himself is how high he wants to raise it. In any aspect of garden design it is important to maintain proportions. In the typical modern small urban garden 2½–3ft (60–100cm) is the maximum rise

from the level that may be achieved and still retain the balance. The higher the water has to be raised the more powerful the pump that will be needed; this will affect both the initial costs and the running costs.

When it comes to siting water features, it is possible to date the building of the garden from certain details. Up until recent times fountains were always sited at the centre of the pond, with no other position being considered suitable. Modern design allows for a far greater degree of individuality and features are now placed at the discretion of the creator. The water garden should be seen in terms of a picture where the eye will slavishly travel to a position one-third of the way into the scene. Ideally, a fountain should occupy a position two-thirds of the distance from the foreground, where the pond is constructed along a direct line from the point of observation to the back of the plot. Where the construction is at 90 degrees to this line then the split should be one-third to two-thirds from either end.

Outlets

The outlets for falling water are many and varied. Once the water has been raised it will of course fall, and you are free to direct it to do so in any way that you choose. Each year accessory manufacturers have become more ingenious in their designs, with tumble trays, watercourses, water dispensers and fountains, and the kits to make them becoming available. In addition, the home handyman may create his own effects, from the classical to the ultramodern, from the obvious to the ingenious.

Pumps

All water is lifted by means of a pump, which draws the water through the inlet, to which a filter must be fitted to ensure that there is no danger of the system being blocked by debris. A piston then pushes the water out under pressure. The height to which the water will

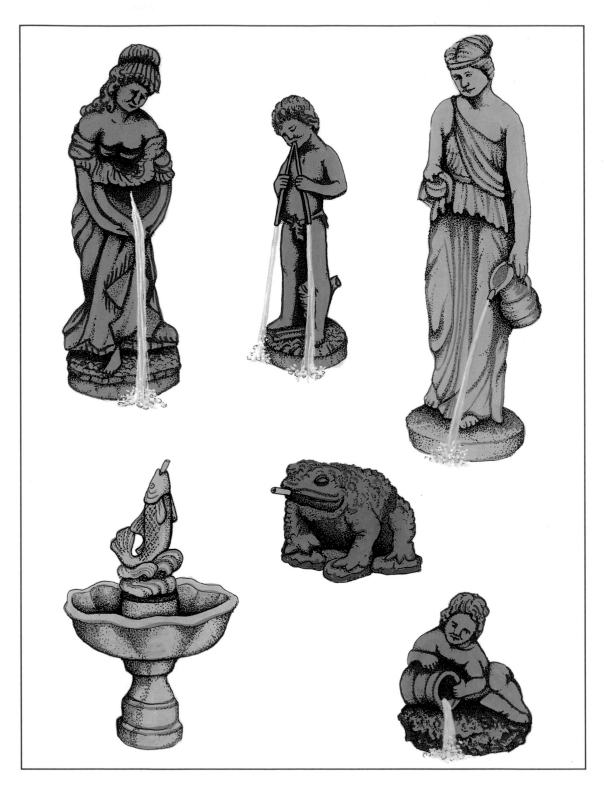

Fig 79   Many and varied are the fountain ornaments that are available.

82

rise will depend upon both the pressure and the size of the hole through which it is being forced – the smaller the diameter of the hole, the higher the jet will rise. Relatively great height may be achieved with a fountain, less with a waterfall. If you are using very small holes to produce height in a fountain, it is important to check that the jet is clear after it has been out of use for any period. Algae and other forms of growth will cause blockage, so be prepared to service the equipment regularly.

For a watercourse it is necessary to raise a large volume of water, to produce the desired audible and visual effects. It is possible to use the same pump for both waterfall and fountain. A 'T' junction is fitted at the outlet; this leads via tubing to the fountain and waterfall inlet, which should be capable of independent control. This has the advantage of simplicity in the majority of garden schemes, but the disadvantage for the more ambitious gardener is the back pressure created at the fountain outlet, together with the extra demand of the two outlets. This means that neither feature is as spectacular as it would be if it were run independently of the other.

Moving water should not be over-done. Not only can it be visually confusing, but the demands can be far greater than the pump can

Fig 80   A watercourse created with simple, rough-hewn logs.

handle, and this will shorten its life. An effective small watercourse will require the raising of hundreds of gallons of water per hour and this will only be achieved if the pump is the correct one for the job. There are so many different types of waterfall and pump that it is essential to seek advice preferably from the place where you intend to purchase the equipment. A long-established reputable dealer, or one of the increasing numbers of garden centres that are providing specialist water garden sections, will be able to advise you on your individual requirements. Gardens are creations that need individual and unique consideration and planning, so it is essential that you discuss your requirements at the design stage. Do not delay until part of the water garden has been built or you might find that what you wished to achieve is impossible, or will be far too expensive in initial outlay or running costs. Only by careful planning will you avoid later disappointment.

Before you visit a supplier it is advisable to understand the difference between the two main types of pump on the market.

Surface Pumps   The surface pump is situated outside the pond itself, and one of the main problems associated with it is the housing it needs to protect it. This has to be near to the water to reduce the inlet length of pressure tubing, and yet in such a position that it does not create a visual intrusion which could spoil the whole effect. Concealment by means of rocks or strategically-placed permanent plants should be sought.

Submersible pumps   These have the advantage that they are simply placed in the pond itself, eliminating the need for both inlet tubing and housing. The pump should be placed on a permanent level structure as near to the surface of the pond as possible, but where there is no danger of the inlet becoming exposed which could lead to an airlock in the system. Do not place it too deep in the water. For any pump, the height which it will be capable of raising a fixed volume of water will

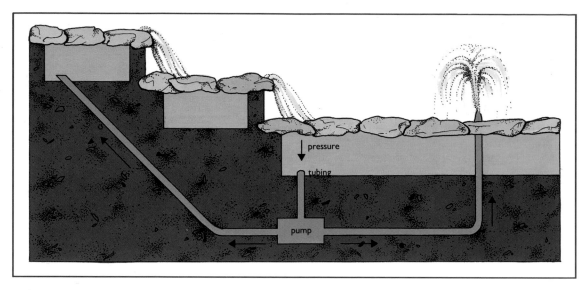

Fig 81   The flow of water, using a surface pump to create a watercourse and a fountain simultaneously.

be limited, and to achieve the most dramatic effect the largest amount of the lift should be created *above* water level.

Submersible pumps present no problems and for small water movements are probably the most convenient.

However, where large volumes of water are to be moved through a relatively great height, surface pumps have the advantage.

Fitting of Pumps

For a pump to function with the greatest efficiency it is essential that the correct hoses and fittings are used. It is also almost as important to ensure that water is moved through the minimum distance in the horizontal plane as in the vertical. Any movement means that the water will have to move against the friction of the system, and the resultant drag will make demands on the total performance of the pump, causing it to be less effective in raising the water. This factor must be taken into account when siting a surface pump in order to maintain maximum efficiency.

Splash Trays

The size of your garden and the need to lift the water will restrict the height of the waterfall. The most effective way to use water is to have two trays with lips over which the liquid will cascade. Trays like this will produce the greatest effect in terms of the water moved, but it is important to ensure that they are situated in a position where they will be lost in the general background. Whilst the two-tray approach is the simplest of all waterfalls, the most complex is little more, using the same cascading trays camouflaged as part of a grander scheme. The observer is mislead into believing that this is a watercourse flowing naturally through the terrain. You must be careful not to end up with an insignificant trickle, and for this reason the cascading trays need a small yet definite functional lip over which the whole of the flow is directed. This results in the most sound and the best visual effect for the volume of water being moved.

Cascading trays may be purchased in a variety of plastics, and you should choose a set which

Fig 82 *Rocks and water coming together to produce an easily maintained part of the garden.*

does not possess too artificial an appearance. Where the trays are completely hidden within the design, the material is far less important. One design which is becoming increasingly popular is where there is a mound of earth, with two trays, a pond and medium-sized pieces of rock placed in the soil. A large variety of plants may be grown in the intervening space. In such a design the appearance of the dropping trays themselves is particularly important, and if you cannot obtain trays that blend visually into your scheme, you should consider making your own. The trays themselves need to be about 3in (7.5cm) deep so that they can hold sufficient water. Make a suitable mould,

and mould the trays (which need to be about ½in (1cm) thick) from a mixture of two parts cement, one part sand, peat or soil to blend with the surroundings, and four parts fine sand. Experiment with different blends – providing the cement ratio is maintained you may adjust the amount of sand and fillers until you obtain the shade you require. Where you are using a soft sandstone for the rock part of this may be ground down to produce the correct shade. Ensure that the trays have lips 2–3in (5–7.5cm) in length, protruding ½in (1cm) over the side. Where cement-based trays are being used it is important to realise that they are liable to breakage as a result of the action of frost;

85

rainfall should be emptied out of them during the winter months to avoid this problem.

Setting up the Trays

You will need two trays in addition to the pond itself. More ambitious schemes involving extra trays will almost certainly be impractical in the small garden, both in terms of visual effect and the expense of installing and running a sufficiently powerful surface pump. The hose from the pump will deliver water to the top tray, which is the smaller of the two, set at 8–12in (20–30cm) above the intermediate tray, which should be at a similar distance above the pond. It is very important that the two trays should be set absolutely level into a firm base and care should be taken to ensure that they cannot move. If necessary, they can be locked into position by the strategic placing of stones underneath.

Waterfalls

Although such a feature is contrived, it will never appear so artificial as to be out of place in any garden. However, should you wish to have a setting which appears almost completely natural, a full waterfall must be built. The mechanics of lifting the water and allowing it to fall will be the same, but the presentation will be different. Build a mound to the back of the pond where you wish the waterfall to be constructed and ensure that it is firm. Any movement as a result of subsidence at some stage in the future could result in the total destruction of the watercourse. The next stage is to cut two steps 8–12in (20–30cm) in depth, and cover these with a 2in (5cm) layer of concrete. The upright sections should be made with shuttering (see page 33). Whilst the cement is still wet the cascading trays should be placed in position, and surrounded by rocks, both for concealment and to create the illusion of a mountain scape. There are several variations on the theme that you can create.

Fig 83 A useful fern for providing greenery is Athyrium filix femina.

The combined effect of the pond and the falling water creating its own vapour is that the air in the immediate vicinity is moisture-laden – the ideal microclimate for cultivating ferns. Ferns are amongst the oldest and most curious plants that have survived on the planet. They do not form seeds, but propagate themselves from a more primitive reproduction system – spores. These can be purchased from many seedsmen and are grown in a similar manner to seeds. Established ferns may be grown in pots and placed by the side of the waterfall, and then brought inside during the winter. The hardy varieties may be planted in a permanent position.

Moving Water and Life

Fish will be attracted to water containing the maximum amount of oxygen, and they will tend to congregate near to a fountain to take in the air-enriched liquid. However, they must be able to spend the majority of their life in still water. Where moving water is included in a small area, such as the two heights of a patio, it may not be possible to provide the necessary environment for the fish. A sufficiently large area of water, on the other hand, could well be out of balance with the overall scheme. Irrespective of whether the water is still or moving, the fish must be provided with a place where they may shelter away from the direct sunlight. This may be provided by including an overlay, or placing a land drainage pipe or half a large flower pot at the bottom of the pond. Where two or more ponds are inter-connected the fish will be able to retreat between the connecting pools.

Plants do not generally prosper in moving water – many subjects which grow in rivers never succeed many feet away from the banks. At the river bank the rate at which the water flows is far slower than it is at the centre, due to the natural drag.

LIGHTING

As gardens become smaller the tendency is to appreciate them more, and to seek ways to maximise the pleasure that can be derived from them. Sitting out in the evening from July through to September can be greatly enhanced by floodlighting the pond. Providing that you buy floodlights that are purpose-built for gardens, the installation is simple. However, *do* recognise the dangers of the combination of water and electricity and employ a competent professional. With a little experimentation and adjustment you will soon find the position which gives you the best effect, showing the water garden to its best advantage, making everything seem more spectacular, and creating magical reflections in the water. One of the best advantages of lighting a garden is the fact that you can sit and watch the numerous caddis flies and moths on the wing, and enjoy the

beautiful evening perfumes of honeysuckle, stocks and *Nicotiana*.

BRIDGE BUILDING

A bridge within a water garden is symbolic, separating one part of the water garden from another, and giving an impression of mass and a degree of cohesion to the whole. Bridges do not demand vast areas nor deep water to span, but simply serve the same purpose as the pergola in a dry garden, linking two distinct parts. A bridge will only achieve this if it is built between, say, the foreground and the backcloth, or a grassed area and a bog garden, and it will not work in visual terms if it is constructed purely as an ornament. This does not mean in practical terms that the bridge should be the sole access to a particular part of the garden. It is far preferable to use the bridge only for occasional journeys (especially if you do not feel confident with the brick or woodwork necessary to produce a full load-bearing structure!). With small water gardens you may build a bridge in proportion, and it may be totally impractical to use as a garden thoroughfare.

Consideration must be given to the materials of construction, which must harmonise with the facade of the house, the outbuildings and, if appropriate, the materials of the water garden itself. A wooden bridge will fit into all schemes, and there are basically two types – planed wood or rustic. With its more regular shape and the greater ease with which it can be preserved, planed wood is the best in the majority of cases. The uprights are easier to construct with sufficient mechanical strength and they are less inclined to become rickety as they get older. Safety and the avoidance of accidents must be a major consideration in the building of bridges. A bridge is an all-weather structure, which must be capable of withstanding the ravages of the elements. Second-hand timber from a demolition site is ideal. Not only will it be far cheaper than the equivalent new

87

Fig 84   *A total pond concept adaptable to all but the smallest gardens.*

material, but you can be assured that it is well seasoned – an important factor. Rub any excessive roughness smooth with a sanding attachment to the electric drill, and fill any nail holes with putty – they will be totally invisible when the wood is covered with preservative.

The framework of the bridge should be bolted together to ensure maximum strength. The floor of the bridge must be made from ¾in or thicker boards, and the structure above the floor may be either 2 × 2in planed wood or rustic poles – larch is the most usual.

Wood above water will be constantly damp, creating the ideal conditions for rot and fungal infections, so it is imperative that the wood is constantly inspected and treated with preservatives. This year's neglect will lead to next year's decay. There are many different wood preservatives on the market, which will all produce a different shade; it is better to seek out a natural shade than the stark black of the old-fashioned creosote. Rustic finishes present a special problem as much of their charm is due to the presence of the bark. This soon comes away from the wood and, whilst preservative is

readily absorbed, this does nothing to protect the layer below which is responsible for the strength of the structure. This layer will be particularly vulnerable to attack by woodlice and honey fungus. With rustic constructions it is far better to remove the bark first wherever this is possible, or as soon as it is practical. All wooden structures should also be inspected regularly to ensure that the joints are secure – this will avoid the possibility of any accidents.

The bridge may have a suggestive role in which it creates an illusion. In the ornamental garden, for example, plywood may be placed on the sides of the wooden bridge and painted with a design. This is particularly appropriate if you are attempting to produce a Japanese garden. This type of garden can be enhanced by the addition of a pagoda, which can double as a purely functional device, such as a shed or store.

Very elaborate brickwork structures may also be created, but building an arch is one of the most difficult skills of a bricklayer, and you should not attempt it unless you are proficient. One of the most sympathetic of all structures is

Fig 85   Providing that you construct a strong base and floor, bridges can be
made load bearing with a variety of different side structures. Here a
rustic design is used to fit in with a cottage or informal garden.

Fig 86   A wooden bridge adds character to this garden pond.

Fig 87   A large flat stone cemented to pillars constructed from smaller pieces of stone make a very effective scenic bridge.

a small stone bridge reminiscent of one of the little bridges across a Pennine stream. However, this again should not be attempted unless you have the necessary experience.

One very simple structure to build has a pillar on either side of the water, created out of rock cemented together in sheets. A plank is placed across the pillars and the level checked with a spirit level (any slight errors can be corrected later by adjustments to the thickness of the cement layer). Next, a large sheet of granite about 2in (5cm) thick is placed across the two pillars and cemented in position, and the level is then checked again. Whilst such a structure gives the illusion of a primitive rock bridge in either an alpine or a Pennine-type landscape, it will not be safe to walk on.

Any maintenance or repairs that are necessary from time to time will be best effected by placing planks across the water adjacent to the bridge, and working from these.

STEPPING STONES

These are an alternative to a bridge – a path through the water – and may be created by anyone. Even when dealing with the shallowest water, you should place them in position before putting the water into the pond. It is possible to construct stepping stones from any depth, but there is always an element of danger. The moist conditions will encourage the growth of micro-organisms and the stones will soon become slippery. Ensure that the water on either side is as shallow as possible if they are to be used for crossing. Where you do not want to use the stones, the only consideration is the visual effect, then the stones and water may be as deep as you like.

A straight line is the shortest distance between two points, and one of the aims with stepping stones (or any type of path) is to give the illusion of length – the impression that the aquascape covers a greater area than it really does. The eye will follow the line of the stones rather than seek out the shortest distance, and it is this that gives the impression to the observer that the area is larger than it really is. The effect can be achieved by laying the stepping stones in an almost straightened-out letter 'S' configuration, with the long backbone traversing the water diagonally and in the process joining the two focal points of the area.

CHAPTER 7

The Water Garden Month by Month

JANUARY AND FEBRUARY

Although there is still very little life in the garden at the beginning of the year, the first bulbs, snowdrops, crocuses and the earliest narcissi are beginning to appear on the scene; the dogwoods provide red coloured twigs. Winter-flowering cherry, witch hazel and winter jasmine vie with the less spectacular *Viburnum* for attention. The background and the surrounds rather than the water garden itself sustain the interest at this time of the year, and emphasise the importance of planning a garden for the whole year and not just for a part of it.

During the bright days bees will stop at the pond for the water that they need to dilute their stored honey before they can eat it, and birds will be seen gathering the materials for their nests. Even though the air is beginning to warm up, the water will be at a lower temperature. Do not be tempted to feed the fish yet – they will probably not take the food, and if it is allowed to remain it will begin to decay. Occasionally there will be mild spells during the winter months and these will become more frequent in the future. The water will get warmer, and the fish will begin to show increased activity and will sometimes take small quantities of food. However, it is by no means essential to feed them. Late winter is very much a time for waiting and watching!

Whenever the weather allows you, take advantage of the situation and perform general tidying-up operations. Weatherwise, this is the

Fig 88 Remember to maintain the water garden during winter.

coldest part of the year and it is the time when ice is most likely to be a problem (see November and December). All equipment – pumps, hoses and jets – should be checked to ensure that they are working efficiently, and any repairs should be done now rather than waiting until the summer. The pond must be regularly inspected to ensure that there has been no sudden drop in water level; should this occur, it is almost certainly due to the pond having sustained a leak. During the dark days of winter plan your display for the borders for the following summer. Border subjects, both wet and dry, can be extremely expensive, and it is possible to grow most of them from seeds. Indeed, seeds for the less common plants can often be purchased from specialist suppliers, even if the plants themselves are unobtainable. They may require some artificial heat at the germination stage and should be started in a warm greenhouse or propagator at the beginning of the year, the actual time depending upon the species.

MARCH AND APRIL

The first sign that the winter is over is the emergence of the yellow cups of the marsh marigolds. The fish will become more active and soon take their first food. All animal life is at its weakest at this time of the year, as a result of having depleted their stores through the long barren months of winter. There will still be a shortage of natural food, but nature begins to take on a sense of urgency, with change becoming more and more apparent each day. The lowest members of the feeding chain breed first, followed by the higher forms of life. Breeding itself requires large quantities of food, and unless the parents can be brought into a peak condition, it is unlikely that many young will be successfully reared. Moreover, when the

Fig 89   Marsh marigold – the herald of spring. The brown spikes are the previous season's growth of reed mace left to show the relative positions of the shorter and taller subjects in the bed and the manner in which the continuum of interest develops from the front to the back.

Fig 90   A spring bog garden with Lysichitum americanum *and young fern fronds.*

animals are in this state, they are at their most vulnerable to disease, and it is at this time of the year that fish are most liable to fungal infections. The time at which the fish will first take food will depend upon the temperature of the water. As soon as any increased activity is noticed, try the fish with a small quantity of food, then give them all of the food that they will consume.

Water Change

Where pools have become polluted, as a result of decaying vegetation or some other cause, a change of water will be necessary. This is most conveniently accomplished by first removing any dead or decaying material and then pumping out or manually removing one-third of the total volume. This should be performed by drawing the water from the top of the pond so that it does not upset the aerobic/anaerobic

balance. The volume of water may be made up with tap water, but this may contain chlorine and other chemicals. It is far better to collect rainwater and store it in a butt (see page 46) and then use that. Whatever the source of the water, it should be added through a hose-pipe at no more than a steady trickle. The fish can safely remain in the pond during the operation.

Frogs will make their way to a natural pond during March and their croaking may be heard during the evening. Eggs will be seen shortly afterwards. If you do not have frogs visiting your pond, and you are intending to introduce a population, this is the stage at which to do it.

By March the worst of the winter's weather should be over (but late frosts may still occur during the next two months), and any of the previous year's growth which remains on the marginals should now be removed. Remove the dead, brown paper-like growths of the

Gunnera which were used to protect the plant through the winter, and generally tidy the margins and bog garden. Many bog garden subjects can still be raised from seeds and, depending upon the variety, can be germinated at this time of the year. Unless you live in a particularly exposed area, any frost after the first half of March should not be sufficient to freeze the pond solid for several days, and any pond heater may safely be removed.

MAY AND JUNE

Daylight, the most important factor in a plant's growth, is now at its most extended and, as water plants have no hardwood, this is the ideal time for planting new varieties. It is also the time for performing the equivalent of weeding in the terrestrial garden. If they are unchecked the water plants will spread and gradually take over the pond. Take out the plants and re-plant, or allow just enough to remain to create the effect which you are seeking. The best time to perform this operation is the second week of May in the south of Britain and a fortnight later further north. Do not delay planting any later than this. Although plants will appear to compensate for lost time, the apparently inactive stage immediately after planting can be the most important in a season's growth. Any plant, whether aquatic or terrestrial, that is delayed will not prosper to the same extent as those which are planted at the correct time.

Delay the planting out of tropical water-lilies, water chestnuts and water hyacinths, and the placing outside of tender fish, until there is no longer any danger of late frosts.

Fig 91   A water garden with a subtly toned colour scheme.

Fig 92   The stately iris commands the margins in June.

itself and the toxic level will gradually build up. Sprays should only be used if they are absolutely essential, and you should seek out one which is not harmful to fish. Aphid attacks, which have been very much on the increase in recent years, can cause considerable damage to water-lilies. Keep a constant look-out for this sap-sucking insect which, in addition to taking the life juices from the plant, leaves the weakened growth open to further infection. This often does far more damage than the insect itself. Pick off any leaves that are infected as the problem will rapidly spread and may destroy even the strongest plants by the end of the summer. With severe infections the leaves may be subjected to a jet of water sufficiently strong to wash the pests into the water, where they will be eagerly snapped up by the fish.

Keep a constant look-out for fish eggs and fry, and transfer them as soon as possible to an aquarium or a pond where there are no fish. The temperature of the water will be rising daily and the oxygen supply will be at its lowest at a time when the fish will be at their most active. Provide additional oxygen by running the fountain or waterfall at least during the morning, or providing a small air pump. The bog garden will dry out unless it is watered regularly, or unless the pond is being intermittently fed with water from the guttering overflowing into it. Even with the latter approach, the amount of water that the garden receives could be insufficient in times of drought or other prolonged periods of low rainfall.

Insect pests will be at their most numerous during this time of the year. Although some plants are liable to attack it is far better to rely on natural predators than to use insecticides, which will also kill insects that are essential to the ecology of the pond, providing important fish foods. The chemicals will fall into the pond

JULY AND AUGUST

Although the summer solstice has passed by now, the momentum for growth will carry the activity through this period. By now the early-season flowering plants will have set seeds, but there are still many late-season subjects to retain interest. Fish may continue to lay eggs right to the end of August although the later broods are not usually as prolific as those of the main season. The fish fry can still be raised in an aquarium. Keep a constant look-out for any over-crowding by the marginal plants, or by the oxygenators, which are also capable of very prolific growth. Dominance by one species must be constantly guarded against as the plants are not only competing for room, but also for the very limited amounts of minerals dissolved in the water.

Should the water-lilies be less vigorous in their growth than in previous seasons it will be due to over-crowding, a lack of nutrients, or a combination of the two. They must be removed and thinned out – a task which can be performed now, but is preferably delayed to the following spring when there are new buds

95

Fig 93 A general view of a water garden in late summer; the dead heads
should be removed before winter.

growing from the roots. They may be fed with a special pond fertiliser pellet which consists of soluble nutrient embedded in clay to keep it at the bottom of the pond. The position at which the minerals are released is important if the growth of clouding organisms is to be kept to a minimum. Provision of minerals is a very critical operation – too little and the lilies will fail to achieve their true potential, too much and the water will not be clear. The best approach is to add less rather than more of the recommended dosage and to provide more frequently. Under no circumstances should you be tempted to add general-purpose fertilisers as these will often result in clouding.

The natural garden will be attracting the greatest variety of different species – moths, caddis flies and other flying insects are attracted towards it, and will find their way to water whether or not you seek to encourage them. In all ponds you may expect to find the larvae of the caddis fly which spins for itself a tube to which it attaches pieces of sand, twig and leaves as a camouflage. This does not stop the goldfish, who find them great delicacies, from seeking them out and consuming them. More likely to survive are the water skaters, which walk across the water using the surface tension. Do not worry if these appear – they are perfectly harmless and just add interest to the water garden.

Of more concern is the growth of blanket or silkweed. The best way to remove this filamentous weed is to place a strong piece of wood in the water and twist it around, simultaneously rotating it around the pond. The threads of the weed will attach themselves to the wood.

Continue to search vigilantly for any signs of aphids, and be prepared to water the bog garden if there is a prolonged drought.

SEPTEMBER AND OCTOBER

Shortening days and lower temperatures mean that all life is beginning to slow down in preparation for the winter. The water garden is still beautiful, with the lilies seeming to acquire a final burst of energy in the early autumn to give one last blaze of colour. Gradually, as the season progresses, there are fewer flowers and the amphibians will have sought out wet stones and other sites where they can spend the winter. The first frosts will blacken the leaves, finally signalling that another growing season has come and gone. Remove the dead and decaying materials from the marginals and take out any excess of water weed that you omitted to trim back in the late summer. Perform these operations as early as is practicable.

Any tender subjects such as tropical water-lilies, water hyacinths, water chestnuts or tender fish should be moved to an indoor aquarium or a tank in a warm (not cool) greenhouse. As soon as the vegetation on the *Gunnera* has died down, use it to cover the centre of the plant – this should be sufficient to protect the slightly tender subject through the winter. Prepare for the falling leaves and the other masses of dead vegetation by placing netting over the pond. Retain this protection until the early spring.

Place the pond heater in position and be prepared to switch it on at the first warnings of a frost, or when it is a clear cloudless night. This is a sure sign of impending frost as the year moves on. If you do not possess a heater, place a large ball in the water. This will not only keep a part of the pond frost-free on nights when it is not too cold, but, during times of extreme cold, it will absorb some of the pressure created by the ice expanding immediately before it melts, and protect the concrete or plastic casing of the pond. If you do not have an overflow system which periodically supplies the water garden with fresh water, remove one-third of the water and replace with clear water (see March and April).

NOVEMBER AND DECEMBER

As each day passes more of what remains of the old year's growth dies. It is at this time of the year that the virtues of either a heather or conifer border are appreciated since they add colour to an otherwise drab garden, and you should now begin planning and executing any major change in the surroundings of the water garden. Many ponds look unattractive at this time of the year because of the general untidiness of the surrounds, so attention must be paid to this if the water garden is the main feature. Keep the beds tidy (weeds still grow during the winter), and mow the lawns, with the mower on the highest setting, when they are neither frosted nor when they are soaked. Do not neglect the garden, but work on the patch whenever the weather allows.

The fish will not take food at this time of the year; their metabolic rate will have dropped to such a level that they will be able to live off the stored fat contained within their bodies. They will also require far less oxygen; much less will be produced by the oxygenating plants, but the cold water will also dissolve more of the life-giving gas from the atmosphere and this will be sufficient for the fishes' needs. The first really cold days usually occur during December. Be on the alert during very cold spells to ensure that the pond does not freeze over completely, because it is the build-up of poisonous gases which cannot escape through the ice, combined with a reduction in the oxygen, which will kill the fishes, rather than the cold. Should the pond freeze over completely, melt a hole in the ice by pouring very hot water into a metal can placed on top of the ice; this will allow the transfer of gases to take place. If you have a pond immersion heater, this may be placed in the hole. Where it is impractical to lead an electrical supply to a pond, you can cover it with a 'tent' of polythene. However, simple structures will seldom be strong enough to withstand the strong equinoxal winds, and should only be used during mid-winter.

97

CHAPTER 8

Indoor Water Gardens

As gardens have become progressively smaller, we have taken them more and more into our homes. A century ago the only subject that was grown inside was the humble pot plant, the ubiquitous aspidistra, but today indoor gardening has become an art. Each year plans become more and more ambitious, with indoor ponds in conservatories, large aquaria in which a wide range of plants are grown, and an increasing number of tropical wetland subjects. If these are to prosper indoors they should be thought of as wetland subjects, and the ideal humidity created, otherwise they will die. The range of indoor wetland subjects is enormous. A small selection is described here, but the list is by no means exhaustive. For example, the bromeliads, some of which contain so much water that frogs can raise their tadpoles in the moisture trapped within the cup-like structures, and the orchids have both been left out as being far too specialist for a general treatment. Included are examples of insectivorous plants, which extract nutrients from the bodies of flies and other insects that they trap to supplement the virtually nutrient-deficient soils, and ferns, once very popular with our Victorian ancestors, which are enjoying a rennaissance. These primitive plants, direct descendants of the primevel world of dinosaurs, are true wetland subjects and worthy of their place in any indoor or outdoor water garden. The choice is almost limitless, and the indoor gardener's problem is in choosing what to omit rather than what to include.

Few aspects of horticulture can offer so much pleasure, or so much interest as the water garden, and it is a feature that may be created in any house, irrespective of its size or position.

Changing architectural styles and ways of life has completely revolutionised the use of plants

Fig 94   The narrow-leaved Marsh Orchid, Dactylorhiza traunsteineri.

in interior decoration. Flat dwellers, and those living in properties with little or no garden, can create gardens inside to compensate for the lack of greenery outside. In the heart of the largest cities are to be found an increasing number of cultivated plants, the majority growing inside properties. The growing of exotic subjects such as the tropical water-lilies was once considered beyond the pocket of all but the wealthiest, but today, with central heating and a little care, the majority of subjects can be grown in most living areas. Landings and other communal areas of flats are now being internally landscaped; many properties incorporate a conservatory, where the indoor water garden is a leading contender for space. The traditional collection of pot plants is no longer sufficient for the modern indoor gardener.

INDOOR PONDS

Indoor ponds will of necessity be smaller than those generally encountered outside. The most practical method of construction is to use a fibreglass liner, although, since the danger of frost damage will be completely eliminated, a concrete pond with appropriate sealer is equally effective. Since there is no danger of weather damage, raised ponds present no problems and represent one of the best approaches to most internal landscaping designs. They are also especially suitable when designing gardens for the handicapped. With all indoor water systems some ancillary heating additional to that afforded by the central heating system must be provided. The central heating system creates a temperature above the water in which the flowers can open naturally. If the ambient temperature is not high enough, the blooms will not open properly and will fail to emit their true perfume. This failure to provide the necessary heat often leads to disappointing results when attempting to grow tropicals. The usual way of growing these plants is to plant them out during the spring to have

them flowering during the summer, when the central heating is not working. However, there is no specific reason why they should be grown in this way. Many of the subjects originate from the southern hemisphere, and December flowering is natural. In the tropics, seasons tend to be far less pronounced, and plants will bloom all year around. You can have some of your plants flowering whenever you choose, providing you take sufficient care to provide the correct level of light intensity – the main factor affecting the growth of plants. This may involve the provision of artificial lighting. The flowering of water-lilies depends to some extent upon the intensity of sunlight, but in this case increasing the length of time of exposure to light beyond the natural amount will only increase the vegetative growth; it will not extend the flowering time, which is fixed genetically.

Indoor water gardening considerably extends the range of plants which can be cultivated. For example, there are heaters designed for outside ponds which will effectively extend the flowering season and allow for the successful growth of the near-hardy subjects such as the water hyacinth, but they are not totally successful with most of the tropical water-lilies. The latter, which include some of the most beautiful members of the genus, must be in a much more friendly environment, and an indoor water garden allows you to do this.

THE AQUARIUM

The use of indoor aquaria to house tropical and cold water fish has long been established, but equally effective results can be achieved when plants are grown in them. Often the only reason for this type of container to fail is because it is too small. Best results are achieved by using an aquarium of at least 4ft (120cm) in length. It is essential to appreciate that the base on which such containers are sited is very important. An aquarium of 4 x 2½ x 3ft

Fig 95   Water-lilies are of course vital to the layout of a water garden.

(120 × 75 × 90cm), filled to within 2–3in (5–7.5cm) of the top, will contain ¾ ton of water. Such a structure needs a brick or concrete foundation. Whilst aquaria of such size tend to be more expensive than ponds, they have a considerable advantage in that it is possible to raise fish *and* observe them. By including both animal and plant life it is possible to create a totally tropical pool environment. Combining both tropical fish and plants requires special techniques. With the fish aquarium it is usual to provide a hood, where the lighting is situated, and which reduces heat losses. Due to the height of many of the marginal plants it is not always possible to use a hood, and in this case other systems of lighting must be considered.

The ideal temperature for a true tropical aquarium is 75°F (23.5°C). This is higher than the comfortable living temperature which is maintained on the average central heating system, and for the best results with the fish it is advisable to fit a special thermostatically controlled heater. These are cheap to buy – in terms of the benefit you will gain from the slight rise in temperature that you are seeking to maintain, the cost is negligible.

Far less oxygen will dissolve in the warm water than in the cold water aquarium, and to maintain the necessary oxygen level you will need to fit a small air pump. These may be obtained cheaply from any tropical fish supplier. It is advisable to incorporate a filter with the air pump in order to maintain clear water throughout the system.

ESTABLISHING THE INDOOR WATER GARDEN

Whether you opt for a pond or aquarium, and warm or cool conditions, the procedure for setting up remains basically the same. The only point to note is that with the aquarium much more attention must be paid to the visual effect from the side. Since the position will be permanent, it is possible to some extent to deceive the eye; flower pots and other containers may be concealed behind rocks so that they appear to be part of the natural scene. Plants grown in containers can be removed from time to time in order to replant or prune back the growths – the restricted size of the indoor structure means that the size that any individual plant can attain is greatly reduced. Those plants to the front of the aquarium must be growing naturally, and this may be best achieved by placing 1in (2.5cm) of peat on the floor of the container, followed by 1½–2in (3–5cm) of pea gravel.

PLANTS FOR THE HEATED POOL OR AQUARIUM

Water-lilies

As with plants for outside water gardens, the most spectacular is the water-lily. It is magnificient in form, with a marvellous scent, and it is well worth considering growing it as a solitary subject apart from the indoor pool. You can do this by growing the plant in an old wooden beer or cider barrel which has been cut in two. Such containers are readily fitted with an aquarium heater and are the equivalent of a flower pot, with the water-lily as the pot plant growing in the water medium. As with hardy specimens, the lilies should not be planted until the spring. Where tub planting is involved the rhizomes are planted into a rich potting medium, while in a large heated pool the method of planting is as for the temperate varieties.

Suitable Species

N. amazona A very large white-flowered species, with blooms up to 4in (10cm) across. It has a heavy seductive scent.

N. capensis This has a bright blue green foliage, but little scent. It grows in 1–2ft (30–60cm) of water.

N. caerulea Known as the Egyptian blue lotus. Delicate pale blue flowers 6–8in (15–20cm) across. Grows best in 2ft (60cm) of water.

N. colorata Although the flowers are only about 1in (2.5cm) across, this is popular due to the delicate lilac blue colour of the flowers. Requires 1½–2ft (45–60cm) of water.

N. mexicana Bright yellow flowers of 3–4in (7–10cm) across. Requires 3ft (1m) of water.

N. lotus One of the largest of all of the species, with flowers over 6in (15cm) across, yet only requires 2–2½ft (60–75cm) of water. Sweetly scented.

N. stellata Blue star-shaped flowers with golden yellow stamens. Requires 2ft (60cm) of water. A spectacular subject, ideal for growing in barrels.

Fig 96 Tropical (indoor) water-lily, Nymphaea 'Blue Beauty'.

Hybrids

African Gold One of the miniature water-lilies ideal for growing in the aquarium, needing only 12in (30cm) of water. It has buttercup-yellow flowers.

Blue Beauty One of the most startling of all water-lily hybrids, with a cup of blue petals encasing a golden centre with blue purple stamens. Only suitable for larger ponds as it requires 3–4ft (90–120cm) of water.

General Pershing Amongst the most dramatic of all water-lilies with very large pink flowers which open over 12in (30cm) above the water. It can be grown in 3ft (1m) of water, although it prefers extra depth.

James Guerney Heavily scented flowers of over 8in (20cm) across. It has very deep pink petals and reddish-yellow stamens, and needs about 3ft (90cm) of water. A night-flowering hybrid.

Missouri Another night-flowering variety, said to have flowers sometimes as much as 18in (45cm) across, although they are usually a little smaller than this. The brilliant white blooms are held above the water.

Nelumbium

Nelumbiums or sacred lotuses are very similar to water-lilies. They are far less well known than the *Nymphaea*, probably because there are no true hardy forms. The leaves, which tend to be very dramatic, are borne on stems which can be from 6–8ft (2–2.5m) in height. The rhizome should be planted in early spring in about 12in (30cm) of water, or even in a pot, providing the soil is always submerged. Unlike the water-lily, the majority of the growth is above the water and these may be considered as tropical marginals. The roots are lifted and stored in a dry place during the winter.

Two species are cultivated – *N. lutea*, which has globe-shaped yellow flowers 6–8in (15–20cm) across, and *N. nucifera*, which has pinkish-red flowers of a similar size.

Panama Pacific is a vigorous-growing hybrid which deepens its colour as it ages. It is a strong grower but only requires about 2ft (60cm) of water.

Cryptocoryne

These species are of eastern origin, and are members of the arum family. They tend not to be as popular in the UK as they are in mainland Europe, and can only be obtained from specialist suppliers, nevertheless, they are intriguing conservatory subjects. They may be grown as wetland subjects providing that their soil is kept constantly sodden. They are not difficult plants, but the success with which you are able to grow them will depend upon the depth of the water and its temperature, which should be about 60°F (15°C). They prefer semi-shaded conditions.

For the beginner, *C. beckettii*, the smallest of all the cultivated cryptocorynes, grows well as a hothouse marginal. Its only requirement is that its roots are constantly submerged. It is free flowering but is valued as much for its foliage as its florescence.

C. cordata, another popular species, prefers moist soils to being totally submerged. Larger species suited for cultivation include *C. willisii* and *C. ciliata*, which may have leaves up to 8in (20cm) in length.

Drosera (The Sundews)

These insectivorous plants grow naturally in bogs and are ideal conservatory subjects. Being mainly of European origin they are not hothouse subjects, but they do need to be grown inside, where their special requirements may be provided for.

The leaves are covered with red thickened hairs, at the end of which is a thick sticky fluid which entraps the small insects; they are attracted towards them, believing that they are a source of nectar. The struggles of the entrapped insects stimulates the hairs to bend to-

Fig 97 *This shallow indoor pool provides an ideal situation for these members of the arum family.*

wards the leaves. These then secrete digestive juices which extract the minerals from the victim. In the impoverished boglands which are the natural home to these curious plants, this is the only way that they can obtain the nitrogen and other minerals that they require. The peaty soil in which they live is deplete of virtually all nutrients, and they prefer a slightly acid soil.

Propagation of these plants is best achieved through the separation of the new plantlets.

Plant the new stock in peat – under no circumstances place fertiliser in the compost or attempt to feed the plants, as this will probably kill them.

There are over one hundred species of sundews. Amongst the commonest in cultivation are *D. anglica* or greater sundew, a plant of the heathlands, and *D. rotundifolia*. Both are low growing, the leaves varying from ½–1½in (1– 4cm) with insignificant flowers of less than 1in (2.5cm) across.

Eichhornia

Eichhornia is also known as the water hyacinth. They may be cultivated outside during the summer months, providing they are brought into the warmth in September. The rhizomes may be planted in the aquarium during the spring (those to be grown in the outdoor pond should be treated in the same manner and only transplanted outside when there is no longer any danger of a frost), and planted in a leafy compost. The pale pinkish-blue flowers appear about three months after planting.

Eucharis

This is a member of the amaryllis family and is not usually considered as a water garden subject. However, it does require considerably more moisture than other members of the genus, and only prospers in wetland conditions. The bulbs, available only from specialist suppliers, should be planted during the spring. Like all members of the amaryllis family it is characterised by trumpet-like flowers which tend to form in clusters.

E. grandiflora is the larger eucharis, with leaves up to 10in (25cm) in length. *E. korsakovii* is the dwarf eucharis, whose leaves seldom grow to more than 4in (10cm) long. Both species need a steady temperature of 60°F (15°C). Your choice should depend purely on the space available.

Kaempferia

These are natural wetland plants that require a very humid atmosphere and will only thrive where this can be created. They have small delicate flowers, faintly reminiscent of the solanums, and rich green leaves which create an almost hosta-like foliage. They perform a similar role in the indoor water garden to that of the hosta outside.

K. pulchra has 6in (15cm) long leaves and is the most suitable species for medium-sized water gardens. *K. rotunda* is twice the size of *K.*

pulchra, and is only suitable for the larger indoor water garden. Where room allows it can provide a spectacular accompaniment to the other subjects. Both are cultivated from rhizomes which should be planted in a humus-rich compost during the spring. Being tropical in origin, they require a constant temperature of 65–70°F (18.5–21°C).

Sarracenia (The Pitcher Plant)

Carnivorous plants are never easy subjects to grow, but the pitcher plants are amongst the most successful in cultivation. The leaves are modified to form an urn or pitcher shape. This holds a liquid which attracts insects by its smell of decaying flesh. Once inside the pitcher they end up trapped in the liquor which contains digestive juices. These extract the minerals that the plant needs from the body of the insect. Pitcher plants may be grown from seed sown in peat compost during the early spring. The growing medium must never be allowed to dry out and the plants should not be fed. Plant the young seedlings individually into pots and transfer the pots to the shallow end of the pond or aquarium. Being of temperate origin (they all come from North America), they may be transferred to the outside wet garden during the summer months. It is essential to ensure that they are not allowed to dry out during this period. Bring them inside during September and keep in a frost-free area. Watering may be reduced during the winter months.

Ferns

Primitive in form, the fern is a true wetland species. There are several species which are temperate, and which can be grown completely satisfactorily outside, but they are usually cultivated indoors as a pot plant. Ferns will survive with little more moisture than is provided by regular watering, but they do need water for their curious mode of reproduction. The plant kingdom is divided into the flowering and non-

Fig 98   *The ever-popular maidenhair fern enjoys a moist atmosphere.*

flowering species, and ferns (and mosses) belong to the second category. Since they have no flowers, they use a means of reproduction which dates back to the days of the primevel forests.

The fern consists of a root, often filamentous and providing little anchorage, stems and fronds. The fronds perform the main function of leaves in the higher plants, in that they generate food and produce spores. When ripe

Fig 99   *The Boston fern is ideal for the indoor water garden.*

spores fall from the fronds into the moist soil. In time they germinate to form a plant that is dissimilar to the parent, called a prothallus. It is this plant which then produces the gametes. If there is sufficient water present, the male sex cell projects itself, by means of its whip-like cilia, to fertilise the female ovum. The new structure germinates and the intermediate prothallus, its role now complete, dies.

It is possible to purchase the spores of ferns, which will germinate to form the prothalluses, and if there is sufficient moisture they will produce the desired forms. Growing ferns in this way can be one of the most rewarding and satisfying of gardening experiences, but you must be patient. It often takes two years to produce new plants in this way. The more usual way of propagating the stock is to divide the crowns of the plants. As with all vegetative propagation this is most successful if accomplished during the spring.

There are several different fern species and related plants. For a detailed description a specialist book should be consulted.

CHAPTER 9

Propagation

Plants may be propagated by one or two methods – sexual or vegetative. The new plant is either generated from only one parent (vegetatively), or by means of seeds in which male and female gametes have combined to form the new plant (the sexual method). Vegetative propagation forms a new plant that is identical to the parent in all respects. On the other hand, seeds of all but species (where the genetic characteristics are the result of natural selection over several years and, except for the very rare mutant, will be constant) are unpredictable. From seeds will come the new varieties, and, very occasionally, new superior forms; the vast majority of the results will be inferior. The crossing of species and varieties should only be undertaken by those who have the patience to wait, and who are prepared to accept disappointments in the hope of one day achieving a solitary variety worthy of recognition.

If you intend to propagate plants on any more than the occasional basis it is essential to set aside part of the water garden as a nursery area, as you might with terrestrial subjects.

VEGETATIVE METHODS OF REPRODUCTION

There are natural methods of vegetative reproduction, which occur as a result of the ability of plant cells (before they are fully formed) to adapt and reproduce themselves to form root cells and hence new plants. The gardener can adapt this natural process to his own needs, and help it by stimulating the cells to form root cells. There will always be some tendency to do this

wherever cells are cut or damaged, but in some instances the plant will die before life-supporting roots can become established. Aquatic subjects, which can take their nutrients through various parts of the system, are often more readily propagated by these means. Growth is stimulated by hormones and the greatest concentration of these will, for all practical purposes, lie at the axil joints where the secondary buds form. Cuttings should always be taken at axil joints and any leaves removed. The division of cells will depend upon both the temperature and the length of daylight, and so, cuttings and divisions should be performed as early in the spring or summer as is practical.

Fig 100   Poolside planting is left to right; Acer palmatum, Polygonum amplexicaule atrosanguineum *and* Iris pallida variegata.

Self Sets

These are new plants which form at some distance from the parent and are the result of a shoot developing and growing from one of the extremities of the root. The new plants are removed and this is the simplest of all methods of propagation, although it has the disadvantage that it will lead to the pool becoming quickly overgrown by the colonising species.

Cuttings

All water plants with elongated leaf axil joints may be propagated by means of cuttings. Your knife must be sharp, as blunt instruments can lead to the damage of several cells within the vicinity of the cut, and rotting diseases setting in.

Fig 101   Cuttings; remove the base leaves so that only one or two remain.

Place the cuttings around the edge of a flower pot – for some reason rooting seems easier at this position. The cuttings need be no longer than 2in (5cm) long, and should be put into a mixture of one part peat, one part well-rotted cow manure, and one part sharp sand or fine gravel. Place the flower pot in a shallow part of the pond. Leave it until the plants have rooted, then plant them into their permanent positions. With all water plants it is better to delay transplanting to the permanent site until they are quite large; this ensures that they will remain at the bottom of the pool. This is particularly important as they do not tend to be deep rooted, and will only overcome buoyancy through the saturation of the tissues with water. This only occurs when the plants are sufficiently well developed.

Division

Crown Division

Plants with crowns have compacted leaf axil joints, and the best way to propagate them is through division of the crowns. Lift a large plant, then place two forks (hand forks for small plants, or ordinary garden forks for large crowns) back to back at its centre. Divide the crown into two by pulling the two forks apart. Whether the new plants are aquatic or terrestrial it is best to place the divisions in a flower pot with John Innes No. 2 or similar compost and allow them to establish roots before they are placed into their permanent site.

Rhizome Division

Water-lilies have rhizomes, which lend themselves to division. These should be lifted in the spring and cut into pieces about 4in (10cm) long with a sharp knife. The pieces are planted into the pool in the same way that you would plant the particular species. Many roots show several eyes, but it is advisable to reduce these to no more than three. The weaker or secondary

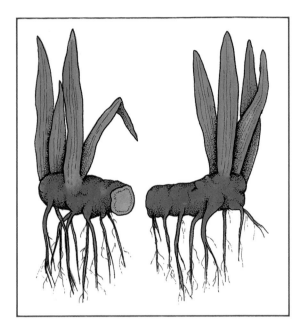

Fig 102 Rhizome division; cut with a sharp knife
and ensure that there are no jagged edges where
disease can set in.

buds will only form inferior growths which will
reduce the vigour of the main shoots.

SEEDS

It is well known that terrestrial plants differ
considerably in their germination periods and
the size of their various seeds. Information is
less readily available concerning the germination
of water plants. In nature the ripe seeds fall
from the parent and may be carried a considerable distance before they settle and germinate.
This usually involves over-wintering in the natural environment. Such methods are wasteful
and, where there is only a limited seed supply,
greater control over the germination is required.

Gather the seeds when they are ripe and
store them in a dry place until the following
spring. This may seem unnatural but it does
eliminate the danger of rotting. No germination

will take place until the temperature is sufficiently
high, so delay planting until the following April
or May. It is essential to be able to see the seeds
without disturbing them.

Prepare an aquarium and fill it two-thirds full
with water. Fill small flower pots with germinating compost. Where the seeds are too small to
handle individually, mix them thoroughly with a
large quantity of white sand and sow the mixture on to the surface of the compost. This will
ensure an even distribution of seeds. Where
large seeds are sown, cover only very lightly
with sand. If the seedlings rise to the surface
once germination has taken place, allow them
to sink – this will occur when the modified stem
structure has had the opportunity to become
full of water. When the seedlings are large

Fig 103 Seeds; carefully cover them with a thin
layer of sand.

enough to handle, replant them into pots filled with growing compost, and allow them to remain in the aquarium until they are large enough for transplanting into their permanent positions.

Germination of Seedlings

Although wetland plants require or can tolerate damp conditions, more seeds and seedlings are lost from damping off than from insufficient moisture. There are two classes of annuals – the hardy variety, which can tolerate frosts, and the half-hardy subjects, which cannot. With all annuals it is important that the young plants are available to be transplanted into their final positions when there is no longer any danger of frosts; this will be late May or June in most areas of the UK. A good early start is essential if the plants are to reach their full potential. The exact planting date will depend upon the species, but many must be started as early as February or March.

At this time of the year it is necessary to provide external heat to bring about germination. This can easily be achieved in any house by use of a small electrically heated propagating unit.

To raise the contents of an average packet of seeds, half-fill a small margarine tub with sowing compost, and then sprinkle the seed evenly over the surface. (Mix very small seeds with sand, as before.) The depth to which seeds must be planted will depend upon their size. Large seeds can produce sprouts that are long enough to push up through the soil, before the plant can support itself by photosynthesis. The seeds of these plants should be sown at a sufficient depth to ensure that they have adequate anchorage.

Some seeds, on the other hand, like those of the begonias, are so small that they can hardly be seen by the naked eye. They contain such a small food supply that the plants must be self-supporting from the moment that the sprout bursts through the seed coat. They should not be covered with any soil or they will perish before they have had the chance to emerge through the soil.

Cover the container with paper until the majority of the seeds have germinated, then remove the paper and allow the seedlings to develop in full daylight. This daylight is very important. If there is insufficient light, the seedlings will be drawn up towards what is available and they will tend to be spindly. The secret of successful seedling raising is to ensure that you achieve strong green growth, rather than the thin weak greenery that is the sign of poor management. When the seeds are about 1in (2–3cm) in length, and are just beginning to show their second pair of leaves, they should be pricked out into a seed box containing growing compost. A standard-sized seed box will hold forty-eight plants in eight rows of six. With the larger subjects such as salvias, which make a most dramatic statement around the pond during the summer months, it is better to plant only half this quantity.

Allow the plants to grow to three-quarters of the size they should be for planting out – 3–4in (7–10cm). With half-hardy annuals you will need to provide some heat during this stage and, if you only have a few plants (perhaps enough for a small town garden), they may be grown on in the propagator. For larger quantities a cool greenhouse or even a windowsill will be suitable for the short period of time that they are at this critical stage. When they are almost at the planting out stage, place the seed boxes in a cold frame and leave the cover off during the daytime. If you do not have a cold frame, simply leave the seedlings outside during the daytime but do bring them in at night. Young seedlings are particularly attractive to birds, especially pigeons; if these present a danger, place the young plants under netting during the daytime. As soon as the danger of frosts seems to have passed – use your own judgement and the weather forecasts rather than set dates – set the plants out into their permanent positions.

CHAPTER 10

Problems with the Pond

The vast majority of pond owners find that it is a relaxing, trouble-free activity, but problems are, of course, occasionally encountered. It is not unknown for a pond to be trouble free for many years and then begin to develop problems. This will be due presumably to some environmental change which is not readily obvious. Fortunately, all problems may be easily overcome.

WATER PROBLEMS

Green Water

Green-coloured water is produced by the presence of millions of algae, or micro-organisms. You will never completely eradicate algae or stop infection, as the windborne unicellular plant is endemic, but you can ensure that the

Fig 104   An example of a healthy water garden with attractive poolside planting.

Fig 105   Beware! The pond holds attractions for a variety of unwelcome forms of life including scum-like algae. A spring-clean is essential if this is not to detract from the beauty.

conditions are not conducive to its growth. It should be considered as a problem which is never solved, but rather as something which must be kept under constant control. A balanced pond life will ensure that there are enough predators effectively to contain the numbers of algae to manageable proportions. Algae require an abundance of mineral salts and light and therefore a large surface area. Where

there are sufficient plants, particularly water-lilies, these will absorb the minerals through their stems, and their leaves will simultaneously reduce the surface area through which the light can penetrate. Until the plant growth has established itself you will never completely cure the problem. Dosage with algaecides will produce only a temporary respite; reinfection will soon occur, and a long-term solution should be sought.

Green water may occur immediately after a pond has been cleaned out, or when the water-lilies have been thinned, or during the spring before the annual growth of the water-lilies has taken place. A fresh supply of compost to the roots or the addition of fertiliser tablets can also cause the problem. Often it is a combination of more than one of these, and it will clear itself.

Black Water

This is an extremely dangerous condition, the result of the decomposition of leaves and other plant materials over the winter period, or a build-up of detritus because of neglect of the pond over several years. It is most frequently encountered where a pond is situated immediately under a large tree. The only cure is to clean out the pond completely and then re-establish it from the beginning. Ensure that plant material does not have the opportunity to enter during future years by putting netting over the pond during the autumn, and regularly cutting back the water weeds.

WEEDS

Blanketweed

This is a green filamentous weed also called silkweed, which will rapidly spread over the whole of the surface of the pond. The best method for the removal of blanketweed is described on page 96.

Fig 106   A large pool covered in duckweed. The plants are primulas and marsh marigolds with rhododendron at the rear.

Duckweed

Although it is no problem in small amounts, once it has become established this floating two-leaved plant multiplies rapidly and if left unchecked it will soon cover the whole pond. It is very difficult to eradicate, but the majority can be easily removed by skimming the surface of the water with a cheap butterfly net, or even a piece of old net curtain stretched across a wire hoop.

STRUCTURAL PROBLEMS

Loss of Water

Any sudden loss of water will be due to damage, either to the bottom or the sides of the pond. This can occur as a result of the action of ice during the winter, through physical damage by a sharp instrument, or because of a flint near the membrane penetrating the liner. The greatest care must be taken to ensure that the

Fig 107   *A pond carefully maintained in winter to avoid structural damage.*

skin is not broken for, although most ponds can be repaired, it is a time-consuming process necessitating the complete re-establishment of the system.

Concrete Ponds

These can usually be repaired by forcing fresh concrete into cracks (the only type of damage that you will encounter with this material). Any new material should be covered with a pond paint to ensure that it is watertight and to reduce the danger of toxins being leached out of the cement.

Fibreglass Ponds

As the name implies, fibreglass consists of strands of glass embedded in a plastic resin. Any break (which may be of either of the types described) will cause most damage to the resin and it is this resin which has to be repaired. Buy one of the kits marketed for repairing holes in fibreglass boat hulls.

Plastic Liners

Almost certainly the damage will result from a sharp instrument as the plastic stretches with the expanding ice. Ensure that you know which plastic your liner is made from. PVC is repaired in a similar manner to a bicycle inner tube. Ensure that the area is clean and dry, rub some talcum powder on to the surface and then, with the aid of a suitable adhesive, stick a patch of PVC of the same quality (cut a piece from the edge if you do not have any available) over the damaged area. Butyl rubber liners are best repaired by means of special self-adhesive tapes obtainable from water garden suppliers.

New materials are constantly coming on to the market and many are designed with repair in mind. Before buying any material from which to make a pond liner, always ask about repairs. You never know when they may be necessary.

FISH

The fish that are recommended are hardy and can withstand the rigours of the British climate, providing they enjoy a suitable environment. However from time to time they do experience problems.

Fish floating on its back   As many people who have kept goldfish in a bowl will tell you, salt is almost a cure-all with these fish. When they are observed in a distressed state, place them in an aquarium with salt at the rate of a teaspoonful per gallon (4.5 litres). This will often revive them.

White cotton-like growths on body or fins   This is due to a fungal infection and must be treated as soon as it is observed, otherwise it will spread rapidly throughout the whole body. Generally it is associated with a fish which has become damaged, especially just after the winter's fast when its resistance to infection is at its lowest. Various proprietary treatments are available for adding to the water. Since the problem is associated with the fish being in a generally low condition, it is advisable to treat all your fish, irrespective of whether symptoms are visible or not.

Rot of extremities and body blemishes These symptoms cover the whole range of tissue-wasting signs which are common for a variety of diseases and are the result of bacterial infections. The treatment is to apply a bactericide – available from a water garden supplier – to the pond water. In this way the problem will be solved. If the fish are taken and treated individually without treating the water, the bacteria will remain in the pond to reinfect and attack the healthy fish.

Fish at the surface of the pond, gulping in air Lack of oxygen is the cause of this problem. This may be due to the temperature being too high, to over-crowding or to a combination of the two. Immediate treatment is to remove the fish and place them in a large tank or bath of water. Turn on the fountain or waterfall, if you have one, to oxygenate the water. The only long-term solution to this problem (which, if left, will continually recur) is to reduce the number of fish or to provide a pump.

MARAUDERS

Herons

Fortunately this is only a problem for rural pond keepers who live near to a river. Herons will soon discover that a pond can provide easy pickings, and the only really effective way to keep them out is to fix 1in (2.5cm) chicken wire over the pond. If this presents a problem a permanent structure must be created which will keep out the herons. This support made from chicken wire or netting can be used to stop the entry of leaves in winter, and will also hold a polythene 'tent' to keep the heat in during the winter.

Cats

This is a far more common problem, as few people live far away from at least one marauding domestic cat. Protect in the same way as for herons.

Fig 108 The grey heron (Ardea cinerea). With modern development robbing the heron of its natural habitat it is fast becoming a serious problem in garden pools only taking a few minutes to devour the complete fish stock.

Insects

Aphids, which appear to be continually on the increase (they now have very few predators as a result of the continual use of insecticides), are the only insects which are liable to cause any major problems. Sprays of any type should be avoided as they tend to be cumulative, and the concentration can build up in the pond or the surrounding environment. The most effective treatment is to cut or break off the infected parts of the plants and destroy them. The insects may be cleared off the leaves by means of a jet of water.

Appendices

I PLANT LISTS

The following lists of plants are those which are readily available and which are generally suited to the situations described. When considering which plants to include in any scheme it is essential that you take all factors into consideration – whether the soil is acid or alkaline, the aspect (whether the plants require sheltered or exposed positions), and the degree of light that is necessary for successful cultivation. It should be appreciated that some plants are tolerant of a very wide range of conditions, whereas others tend to prosper only in environments where their particular requirements can be met.

Fig 109   *The combination of* Primula florindae *and* Iris pallida variegata *produces a pleasing blend of foliage and flowers.*

Fig 110   Aspargus plumosus *(florist fern)*.

Ferns and Related Plants Suitable for Growing Indoors

Adiantum capillus veneris (maidenhair fern)
Asparagus plumosus (florist fern)
Asplenium bulbiferum
Ceterach offinicarum
Nephrolepis exaltata
Phyllitis scolopendrium vulgare (hart's tongue)
Platycerium bifurcatum
Pteris cretica
Seleginella apus

Bromeliad Species

These are essentially indoor plants which can be grown in conjunction with an internal aquascape. They tend to grow in moist conditions, and it is the fogs and mists of the rainforest in which they are at home. In many instances their shallow roots take hold in the general plant detritus which collects in the branch joints and the crevices of the bark. These plants have formed cup-like structures as a result of necessary modifications, trap and retain moisture and should be kept damp by spraying. The roots should also be kept damp, but not soaked.

Aechmea
Billbergia
Cryptanthus
Neoregelia
Vriesia

Aruncus
Astilbe
Caltha palustris
Eupatorium
Gunnera
Hosta
Iris (var.)
Lobelia cardinalis
Mimulus
Primula
Rununculus
Thalictrum
Trollius

Plants for Moist Areas and Margins

For cultivation details please consult the main text.

Water and Marginal Plants

Agonogeton (water hawthorn)
Calla palustris (bog arum)
Caltha palustris (marsh marigold)

Fig 111   Caltha palustris 'Alba', white marsh marigold.

Fig 112 Nymphaea *sp. (water-lily).*

Iris kaempferi (iris)
Iris laevigata (iris)
Mentha aquatica (water mint)
Menyanthes trifoliata (bog bean)

Nymphaea sp. (water-lily)
Ranunculus lingua (spearwort)
Sagittaria sagittifolia (arrowhead)
Typha minima (reed mace)

Plants for a Rock Garden

The following plants may be used in a rock garden built in conjunction with a water garden to provide a range of colour throughout the year.

Alyssum
Arabis
Aricula
Campanula
Cheiranthus
Crane's bill (geranium)
Crocus
Cyclamen (*C. neapolitum*)

Fig 113   A delicately coloured campanula.

Daffodil (miniature)
Dianthus
Gentian
Geum
Helianthemum
Iris reticulata
Narcissus sp. (miniature)
Rhododendron (dwarf species)
Saxifraga
Sedum
Sempervivum
Thyme
Tulip (*kaufmanniana*)

Annual, Biennial and Perennial Plants

The following plants can be grown in beds around water gardens for summer displays. Classification of these plants is not an exact science. Antirrhinums are perennials in that they will continue to flower each year if left undisturbed, but they are usually grown as annuals, with new plants raised each spring and the old removed in the autumn.

Ageratum
Alyssum
Antirrhinum
Calceolaria
Calendula
Campanula
Cineraria
Clarkia
Cosmos
Delphinium
Godetia
Impatiens
Lobelia
Mesembryanthemum
Nasturtiums
Nemesis
Nicotiana
Pansy (summer and winter)
Pelargoniums
Phlox
Primula

Fig 114   *Pelargoniums are a useful bedding plant for added summer interest.*

Salvia
Stocks
Tagetes
Zinnia

Dwarf Conifers for Rock Gardens near Pools

Virtually all dwarf conifers are ideal subjects for growing in conjunction with rocks and water. They should not be grown in sodden soil, but their roots, far shallower than those of the larger species, must be provided with water during the summer months. Amongst the best species and varieties are:
Chamaecyparis obtusa
Juniperus horizontalis
Picea abies
Pinus sylvestris 'Beuvronensis'

Fig 115   Dwarf conifers add interest to a winter bed.

Waterside Trees and Shrubs

Acer palmatum
Azalea
Birch
Box
Cistus
Cotoneaster

Hebe
Magnolia
Malus
Potentilla
Prunus (cherry, plum and almond)
Rosa (some sp.)
Viburnum

Fig 116   Acer palmatum, *an ideal tree for growing near to ponds.*

Fig 117   *Azaleas will brighten up any border.*

Fig 118   Viburnum, displaying striking green leaves.

Spring-flowering Bulbs

In some instances there are many different species of these bulbs. Unless otherwise stated, all may be considered as spring-flowering subjects.

Allium (some sp.)
Anemone
Crocus
Daffodil
Hyacinth
Iris (some sp.)
Muscari
Narcissus
Tulips

Terrestrial Plants of Medium Height

The following plants are useful for growing behind water gardens.

Delphinium
Flag lilies
Foxgloves
Hollyhocks
Lupins (Russell hybrids)

Fig 119   Heather provides an excellent complement to dwarf conifers.

Pampas grass
Red hot pokers

Heathers

All heathers may be grown in conjunction with dwarf conifers and rocks as part of the back-cloth to a water garden (although some varieties of *Erica carnea* may grow too tall). All heathers require an acid soil; even the so-called 'lime-tolerant' varieties fare much better if grown in peat. To create ideal conditions for this plant, remove a quantity of topsoil and replace with peat before planting. Mulch each year with peat. This will be sufficient for these shallow-rooted varieties. The same technique may be used to grow rhododendrons on chalky soils.

II GLOSSARY

Aerobic   Normal manner in which organisms respire, breaking down carbohydrates with oxygen to liberate energy.

Anaerobic   Respiration without free oxygen; the oxygen contained in the carbohydrate itself is used to liberate the energy, in a far less efficient process than aerobic respiration.

Alpine   A rock plant, or apertaining to a rockery.

Batter   The angle at which a retaining wall or sloping pond wall is built.

Calyx   The collection of sepals on a flower.

Carbohydrate   A chemical compound containing carbon, hydrogen and oxygen only. The hydrogen and oxygen are present in the same proportions as in water. This is the material that the plant uses to store its energy (starch), and cellulose, which is necessary to provide mechanical strength.

Cultivar   A distinct variety.

Form   The height, mass and shape of an organic feature such as a tree, or of an inorganic feature such as a rockery.

Frond   The leaf of a fern.

Genus   A collection of species which make up a known plant such as a water-lily. Species of the same genus can usually be hybridised. The genus name is the first word in the scientific name, and it is often abbrievated to just the letter where the context is clear. (For example, *nymphea* is usually referred to in a list as *N.*, followed by the species name.)

Hybrid   The cross produced by two species of the same genus, or a cross involving other hybrids.

Inorganic   Of mineral origin as opposed to natural substances.

Metabolic rate   The speed at which energy is used up by a living organism.

Metamorphosis   The change of one or more forms of a living organism until the adult form results. Examples include tadpoles changing into frogs, or a caterpillar changing into chrysalis and then into the adult insect.

Microclimate   The weather conditions in a very small part of the garden as distinct from the climate in the garden as a whole.

Micro-organism   A living thing which is so small that one cannot be seen by the naked eye, although colonies can be seen.

Microbe   A contraction of 'micro-organism'.

Mutation   A naturally-occurring sport, usually the result of the occurrence of a new gene.

Molecule   Basic single unit of a chemical compound.

Organic   Natural substances (substances which contain carbon).

Oxygen   A chemical element capable of releasing stored energy by respiration.

Petal   A free segment of the corolla, situated inside the sepals.

pH   A scientific scale for comparing the acidity and alkalinity of water. The neutral point is 7.0. Values above are alkaline and those below acidic.

Photosynthesis   The process by which plants produce carbohydrates from carbon dioxide and water, using the energy from sunlight.

Plane of symmetry   In design, where the feature to the left of a line is related to that to the right in the same way that an object and its mirror image are related.

Respiration   The release of energy within the cells of all living things.

Sepals   The outermost component of a flower.

Species   A distinct, naturally-occurring form of a genus. The species name is the second word in the scientific name.

Stagnant   Still water that is hostile to higher forms of life as a result of decomposing leaves and dissolved materials.

Syn. (synonym)   Alternative name.

Tannic acids   A group of chemicals that are very astringent and offer some protection to the leaves from insect damage. In ponds they tend to produce brown coloured water which is slightly acidic and hostile to growth.

Variety   An improved form of a natural mutant of a species; a hybrid.

Index

(Note: Page numbers referring to illustrations appear in *italics*.)

Acer palmatum, *123*
aconitum (monkshood, wolf's bane), 53
algae, green, 14, 20, 43, 83, 111–12
alpine plants: pool with, *58*
　by water, 58–60, 81
amphibians: in water, 78–9
Aponogeton distachyos (water hawthorn), 65
aquarium, 70, 99–100
arums, *103*
aspect, 16, 20
astilbe (spiraea), 53
azaleas, *123*

baskets, underwater, 49, *61*
bedding plants, 6, 121
beetles, 79
birds: and ponds, 7
black water, 112
blanketweed, 112
bog garden: size of, 17
　in spring, *93*
　and water supply, 46, 47
bog plants, 5, 23, 52–7
bridges, 87–90
Bromeliad species, 117–18
brooklime (*Veronica becqbunga*), 77
building: of ponds, 29–42
bulbs: spring-flowering, 124
butyl rubber lining, 35, 114

Calla palustris (bog arum), 62
Caltha sp. (marsh marigold, kingcup), 62–3
　palustris 'Alba', *118*
campanulas, *120*
carp, 66
　Higoi, 7
　Koi, 9, *68*, *69*, *73*
　ornamental, 67
　see also goldfish
cats: problems with, 115
circular ponds, 31

classical gardens, 24–5
climate: *see* microclimate
colour: of water-lilies, 48, 49
　use of, in gardens, 24, *94*
Comet, 72
concrete ponds, 30–5, 114
conifers, dwarf, 59, 97, 121, *122*
containers: grown plants, 20, *32*
　for marginal planting, 60
cottage garden, 21–4
Cryptocoryne, 102
cuttings, *108*

design of garden: and water, 22
　and patio pools, 28
　and pond shape, *34*
　see also planning
dimensions: of ponds, 30–2
division: crown, 108
　rhizome, 108, *109*
duckweed, common, 75, *113*
Drosera (sundews), 102–3
dry borders: by water, 58–60

Eichhornia crassipes (water hyacinth), 65, 99, 104
environment: balance in, 14–15, 47
　creation of, for water plants, 6
　and ecology, 76, 77
Eucharis, 104
Euphorbia palustris, 54

Fantail, 72
ferns, *86*, *93*, 104–6
　Asparagus plumosus, 117
　Boston, *106*
　Maidenhair, *105*
fertilisers: for ponds, 96
fibreglass ponds, 38–40, 99, 114
fish, 9, 10, 18, 66–74, 86–7, 92, 95, 97
　aquarium, 100
　problems of, 114–15
　varieties, *68*
flea bane, *53*
floating plants, 65

formal gardens, 18–20
　layout, *19*
fountain, 28, 74, 80
　in classical garden, 25
　in formal garden, *20*, *29*
　ornaments, *82*
　position, 81
freezing of water, 16, 18, 67–8, 91, 97
　in sink ponds, 41
frogs, 78, 93
frogbit, 65
　see Hydrocharis morsus-ranae

garden design: and pond shape, *34*
　types of, and pools, 18–28
　and water, 4, 9, 10
golden orfe, 73
goldfish, 9, 67, 70
　food for, 71, 72
　types, 72, 73, 74
green colour: use, in classical gardens, 24
green water, 111–12
　see also algae
gunnera, 9, 94, 97
　manicata, 54
gypsy wort, 64

heathers, 59, 97, *125*
　grey, *115*
hosta, 54, 55
Hydrocharis morsus-ranae (frog bit), 65

ice-holes, 68, *69*, 97
indoor water gardens, 98–106
informal gardens, 21–4
insecticides: use of, 6, 95
insects: and ponds, 6, *78*, 79, 95
　problems with, 115
iris, 95
　Kaempferi, 63
　pallida variegata, *116*
　Pseudacorus, 64

Juncus effusus 'Spiralis' (corkscrew rush), 62

Kaempferia, 104

layout: of water gardens, *4, 9, 13, 19*
lighting: flood-, of ponds, 87, 99
liners: for ponds, 35–7
Lobelia cardinalis, 55
Lysichiton syn. *lysichitum*, 55
    Americanum, *93*

maintenance of ponds, 47, *91*, *114*
manure: use of well-rotted, 46, 49
marginal planting, *21*, 22–3, 26,
    60–5, 118–19
    design, 61–2
marsh marigold, *63*, *92*
    see *Caltha* sp.
Mentha aquatica (water mint), 63, *64*
Menyanthus trifoliate (bog bean),
    63–4
microclimate: and position of pond,
    15–16, 18
Mimulus sp. (the monkey flower) 55
    cardinalis, *61*
movement: in water, 80–7
mussels, 79
Myositis palustris syn. *M. scorpioides*
    (water forget-me-not), 64

natural ponds, 29, 75–9
    ecology of, *76*
Nelumbium, 102
newt: great crested, 79
    smooth, 79
Nuphar, 65
nutrients: in pools, *45*, 46
Nymphaea, 50, 52, *119*
    'Nile Beauty', *101*
Nymphoides (floating heart), 65

orchid: marsh, *98*
ornamental gardens, 25–6
ornaments, 9, *26*
oval ponds, 31–3
oxygen: need for, 44–5, 67, 69, 74,
    77, 100

patio: ponds in, 26–8
pansies, *59*
pelargoniums, *121*
Peltandra sp. 64
planning: of water gardens, 10, *12*,
    14, 22

planting scheme, 23–4, *107*
plants, 5, 48–65, 116–26
plastolene lining, 35, *114*
pond heaters, 69, 97
pond life, 66–79
pond liners, 10, 35–7
pond moulds, 10
ponds, 5, 7
    indoor, 99
    irregular, 32
    as part of total garden layout, *9*
    problems with, 111–15
    section through, *35*
    shape of, *8*, *29*, 30–2, *33*
    total concept, *88*
    types of, 30–42
    in woodland, *11*, *15*
position: and planting, 24
    of water garden, 13–16, 18
primula, 56
    denticulata, *56*
    florindae, *61*, *116*
    pulverulenta, *57*
propagation, 107–10
pumps, 81–4
PVC lining, 35, *114*

raised ponds, *41*
Ranunculus lingua 'Grandiflora
    (pearwort), 64
rectangular ponds, 30–1
Rheum palmatum, 56
rock gardens: plants for, 120–1
    and water, *23*, *24*, *32*, *58*, *85*

Sagittaria (arrowhead), 64
Sarracenia (pitcher plant), 104
saucer bug, 79
seeds: propagation, *109*, *110*
self sets, 108
shrubs: waterside, 122
Shubunkins, 72
silkweed, 96
sink ponds, 41, *42*
siting: of water garden, 13–28
size: of water garden, 17–18
snails, 74, 79
spiders, 79
splash trays, 84–6
Stachys palustris (marsh woundwort),
    65

stone: stepping, 90
    use of, 24–5, 60
surrounds: for patio pool, *28*

toads: common, 78
Trapa natans (water chestnut), 65
trees: waterside, 122
Trollius (globe flower), 9, 56, *57*
Typha sp. (reed mace), 65

vegetative propagation, 107–9
Veiltail, 73
viburnum, *124*

waterfalls, 9, 28, 74, 80, 81, 86
    with logs, *83*
water garden: general view, *6*
    healthy, *111*
    history, 9–10
    in late summer, *96*
    month by month, 91–7
    movement in, *81*
    small, *17*
    total concept, *80*
water: changing, 93
    danger of, 12
    quality, 47
    running, *17*
    stagnant, 47
    supply, 46
water hawthorn, 65
water-lilies, 5, 9, 18, 26, 47, 48, 49,
    53, 95, 97,*100*
    dwarf, 42
    in formal gardens, 18, *20*
    hardy, 50
    hybrids, 50, 52–3, 102
    indoor, 101–2
    and planting scheme, 23–4
    species, 50, 52, *101*
    tropical, 99
    varieties, 49–53
    white, *51*
    see also *Nymphaea*
water milfoil, whorled, *75*
water mint, *64*
wetlands, 5, 98, 106
water weeds, 47, 74–5, 112–13
    for oxygenation, 44, 69, 77
winds: protection from, 15, 16

Zantedeschia aethiopica, 65